SONG INDEX

ADORE	1
AW, AW, YEAH	4
ALL MY LIFE	6
ALWAYS AND FOREVER	9
BELIEVE	11
BREATHE ON ME	13
BROKEN	15
COME BEFORE	17
DEEPER	19
EMBRACE THIS PLACE	21
EMMANUEL	23
EVERYTHING	25
EVERYTHING THAT HAS BREATH	28
FAITHFUL	31
GETCHA	33
GIVE IT UP	36
GLORIFY	38
GOD OF GLORY	40
GOT THE NEED	43
HA HEI BEACH	46
HOLY ANOINTED ONE	48
HOLY ONE	50
HOLY SPIRIT	53
HOW I LONG FOR YOU	54
HUNGRY FOR YOU	56
I AM AWARE	58
I FALL DOWN	61
I LIFT UP YOUR NAME	63
I STAND IN AWE	66
I WILL CALL	68
I'M YOUR SERVANT	71
IMMERSE ME	74
IN THE NAME OF JESUS	77
INSPIRED	80
JESUS	82
JESUS, I BOW DOWN	84
JESUS IS REAL	87
JOURNEY CLOSER	89
LET EVERYTHING	92
LET GOD ARISE	95
LET YOUR GLORY FALL	98
LIVING FOUNTAIN	100
LORD OF THE HEAVENS	102
LOVE YA	105
LOVE YOU MORE	107
PLEASE WALK BESIDE ME	109
PRAISE HIM	112
PURE AND HOLY	114
RADIANCE	116
RAIN DOWN	118
REDEMPTION DAY	120
RISE UP	122
SHELTER ME	124
SHOUT IT	126
SO GLAD	129
SPIRIT COME	131
START A FIRE	133
THANK YOU, JESUS	135
TOUCH ME, LORD	138
WAIT ON YOU	142
WE SEEK YOUR FACE	145
WHERE CAN I GO?	148
WITHOUT YOU	151
YOU ALONE	153
YOU ARE GOD	156
YOU ARE GOD ALONE	159
YOU ARE LORD	161
YOU MAKE ME FREE	163
YOU MEAN EVERYTHING TO ME	166
YOUR LOVE	168

SONG KEYS

ADORE	Em
AW, AW, YEAH	B
ALL MY LIFE	E
ALWAYS AND FOREVER	Bm
BELIEVE	Em
BREATHE ON ME	D
BROKEN	E
COME BEFORE	B
DEEPER	C#m
EMBRACE THIS PLACE	G
EMMANUEL	Gm
EVERYTHING	D
EVERYTHING THAT HAS BREATH	C
FAITHFUL	A
GETCHA	Am
GIVE IT UP	Cm
GLORIFY	G
GOD OF GLORY	Bm
GOT THE NEED	Gm
HA HEI BEACH	D
HOLY ANOINTED ONE	D
HOLY ONE	E
HOLY SPIRIT	E
HOW I LONG FOR YOU	G
HUNGRY FOR YOU	Bb
I AM AWARE	Eb
I FALL DOWN	A
I LIFT UP YOUR NAME	F
I STAND IN AWE	Ab
I WILL CALL	D
I'M YOUR SERVANT	D
IMMERSE ME	D
IN THE NAME OF JESUS	Em
INSPIRED	F#m
JESUS	F
JESUS, I BOW DOWN	A
JESUS IS REAL	C
JOURNEY CLOSER	G
LET EVERYTHING	E
LET GOD ARISE	E
LET YOUR GLORY FALL	F
LIVING FOUNTAIN	E
LORD OF THE HEAVENS	D
LOVE YA	F
LOVE YOU MORE	Em
PLEASE WALK BESIDE ME	C
PRAISE HIM	Am
PURE AND HOLY	Ab
RADIANCE	Am
RAIN DOWN	C#m
REDEMPTION DAY	D
RISE UP	G
SHELTER ME	C
SHOUT IT	Dm
SO GLAD	Cm
SPIRIT COME	F
START A FIRE	F
THANK YOU, JESUS	G
TOUCH ME, LORD	C
WAIT ON YOU	A
WE SEEK YOUR FACE	Am
WHERE CAN I GO?	G
WITHOUT YOU	G
YOU ALONE	Am
YOU ARE GOD	Em
YOU ARE GOD ALONE	A
YOU ARE LORD	F
YOU MAKE ME FREE	G
YOU MEAN EVERYTHING TO ME	F
YOUR LOVE	A

PROJECT INDEX

AMONG THORNS:
EMBRACE THIS PLACE	21
HOLY ANOINTED ONE	48
HOLY SPIRIT	53
I WILL CALL	68
LIVING FOUNTAIN	100
RAIN DOWN	118
RISE UP	122
SHELTER ME	124
START A FIRE	133
YOU ARE GOD	156

AWE: "Volume 1"
AW, AW, YEAH	4
I LIFT UP YOUR NAME	63

FORM: "Journey Closer"
BELIEVE	11
BROKEN	15
COME BEFORE	17
GLORIFY	38
HA HEI BEACH	46
IMMERSE ME	74
JOURNEY CLOSER	89
LET EVERYTHING	92
REDEMPTION DAY	120
WAIT ON YOU	142
YOU MAKE ME FREE	163

THE PARACHUTE BAND: "Always and Forever"
ALWAYS AND FOREVER	9
GOT THE NEED	43
HOW I LONG FOR YOU	54
I AM AWARE	58
I FALL DOWN	61
I'M YOUR SERVANT	71
LOVE YOU MORE	107
PURE AND HOLY	114
RADIANCE	116
YOU ARE GOD ALONE	159

THE PARACHUTE BAND: "Adore"
ADORE	1
DEEPER	19
GIVE IT UP	36
GOD OF GLORY	40
HOLY ONE	50
LET YOUR GLORY FALL	98
LORD OF THE HEAVENS	102
PLEASE WALK BESIDE ME	109
PRAISE HIM	112
SO GLAD	129
WITHOUT YOU	151
YOU ARE LORD	161

THE PARACHUTE BAND: "You Alone"
BREATHE ON ME	13
EVERYTHING THAT HAS BREATH	28
FAITHFUL	31
HUNGRY FOR YOU	56
IN THE NAME OF JESUS	77
JESUS, I BOW DOWN	84
JESUS IS REAL	87
SPIRIT COME	131
THANK YOU, JESUS	135
WE SEEK YOUR FACE	145
WHERE CAN I GO?	148
YOU ALONE	153
YOU MEAN EVERYTHING TO ME	166

THE PARACHUTE BAND: "Love"
ALL MY LIFE	6
EMMANUEL	23
EVERYTHING	25
GETCHA	33
I STAND IN AWE	66
INSPIRED	80
JESUS	82
LOVE YA	105
SHOUT IT	126
TOUCH ME, LORD	138
YOUR LOVE	168

*NEW BONUS SONG:
LET GOD ARISE	95

Aw, Aw, Yeah

Key of B

Words and Music by
Jason Harrison and Jay Hall

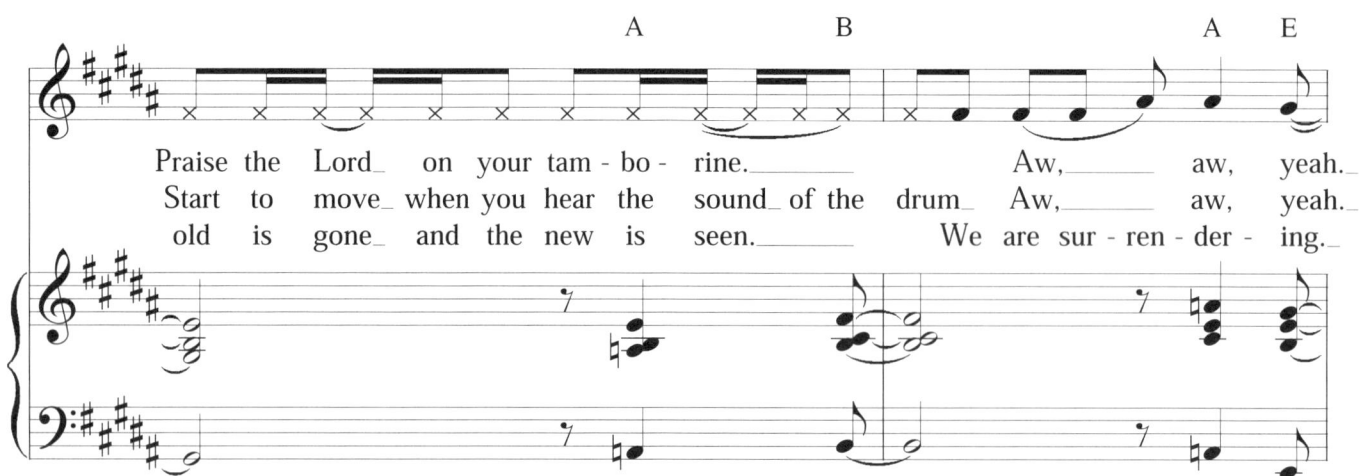

From the Here to Him Music release: AWE (Alternative Worship Experience)
© 2000 ShadowRock Publishing Group, Admin. in the U.S. and Canada by Howard Publishing, Inc., West Monroe, LA
www.worshipextreme.com

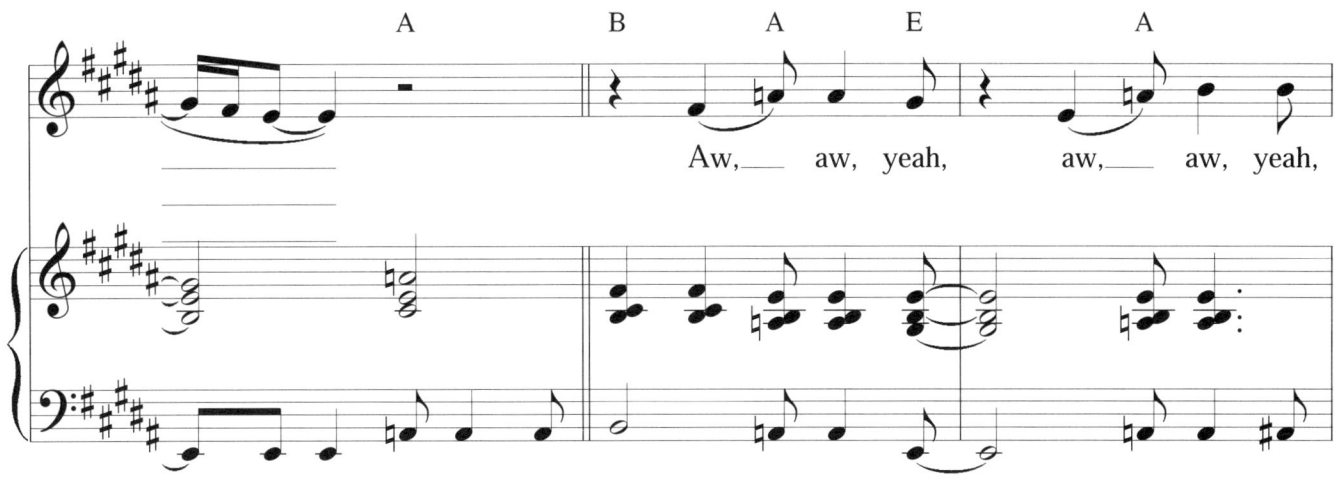

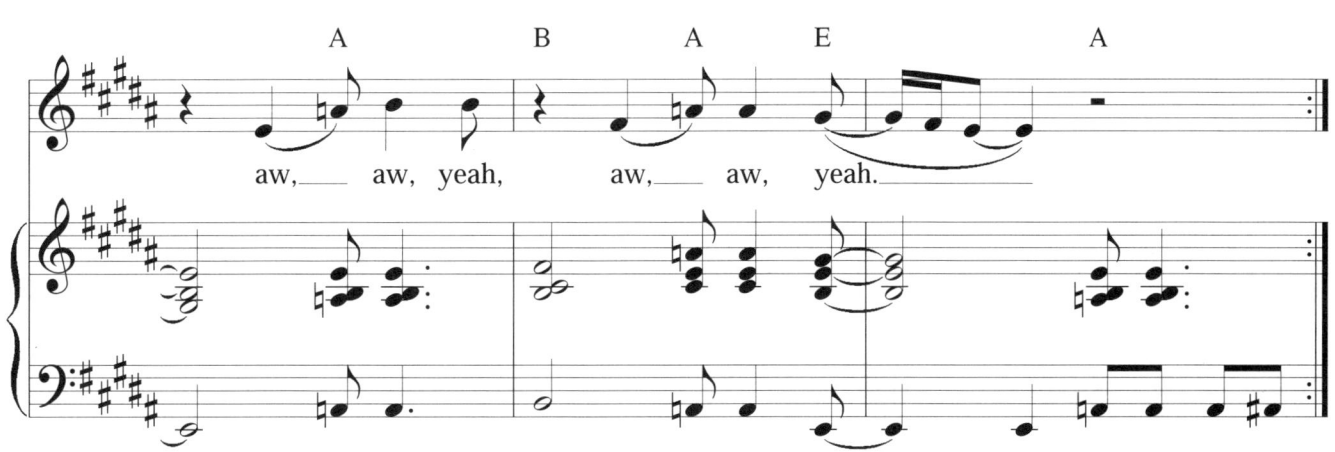

Always and Forever

Key of Bm

Words and Music by
Chris de Jong

From the Here to Him Music release: "Always and Forever" (Parachute Band)
© 1998 Parachute Music, Admin. in the U.S. and Canada by Howard Publishing, Inc., West Monroe, LA (BMI)
www.worshipextreme.com

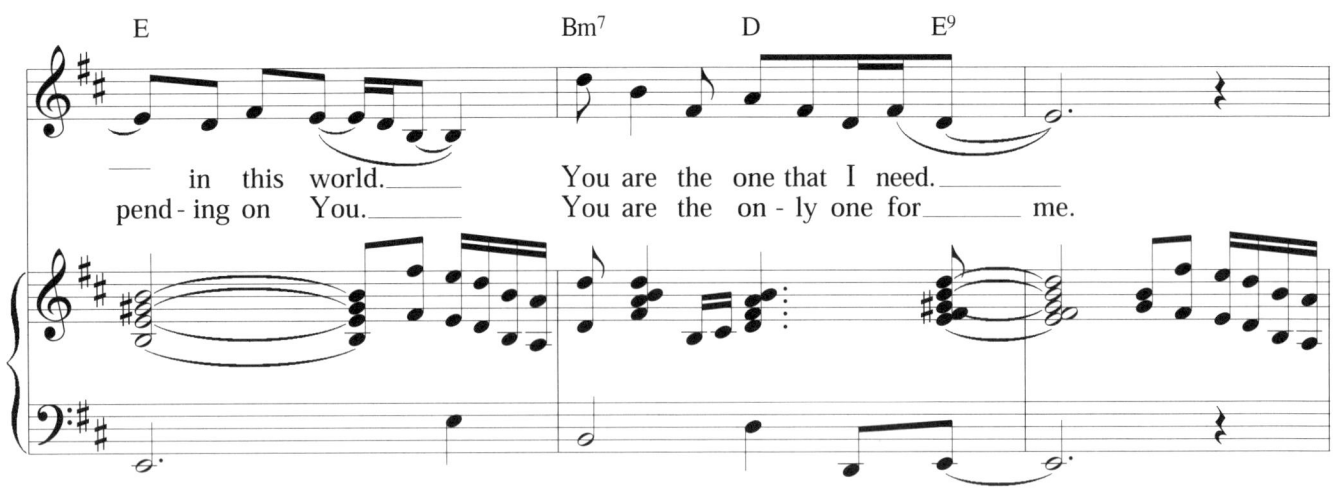

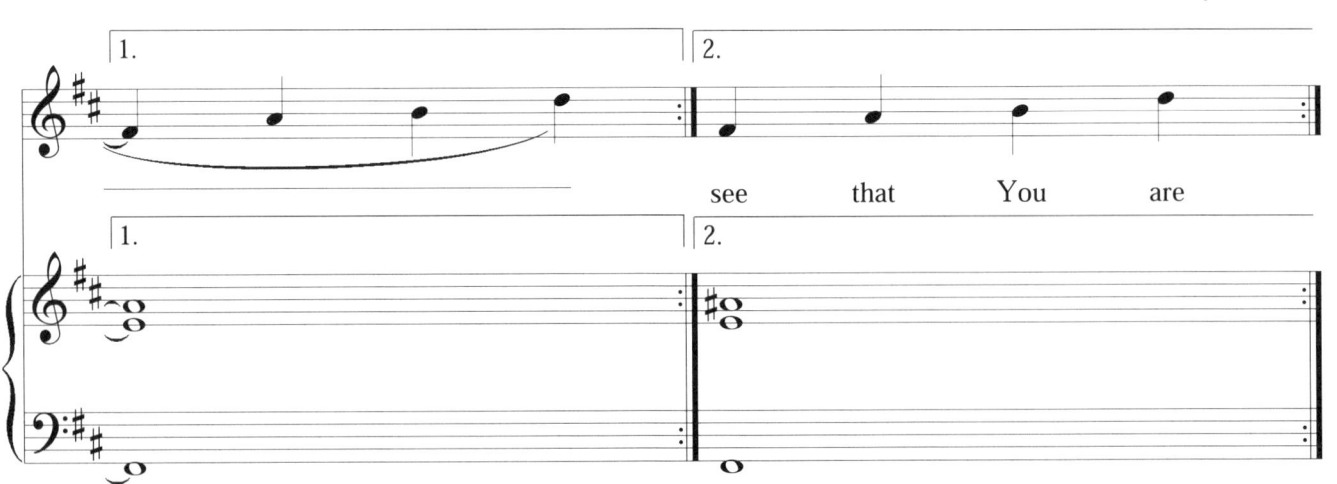

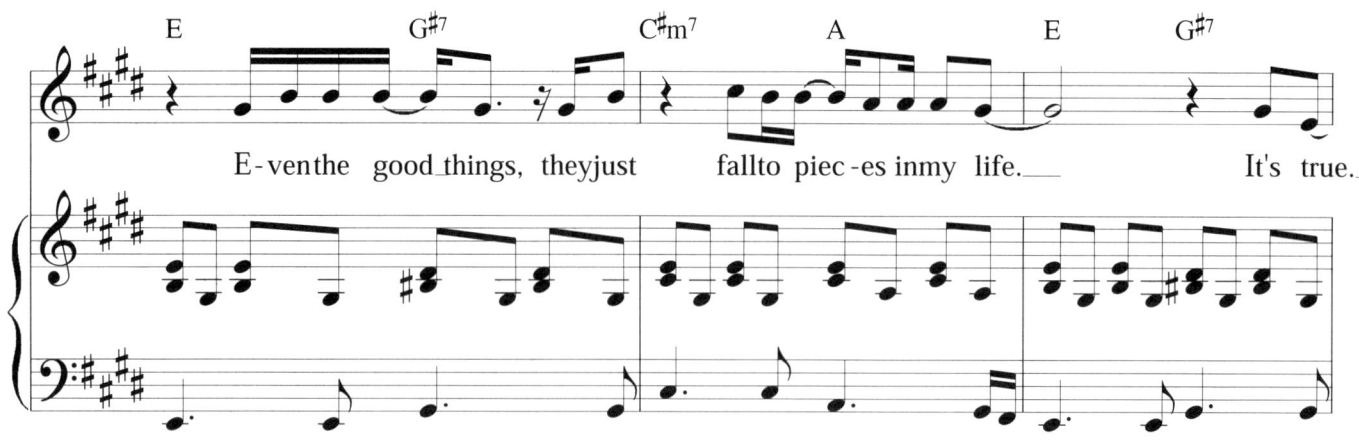
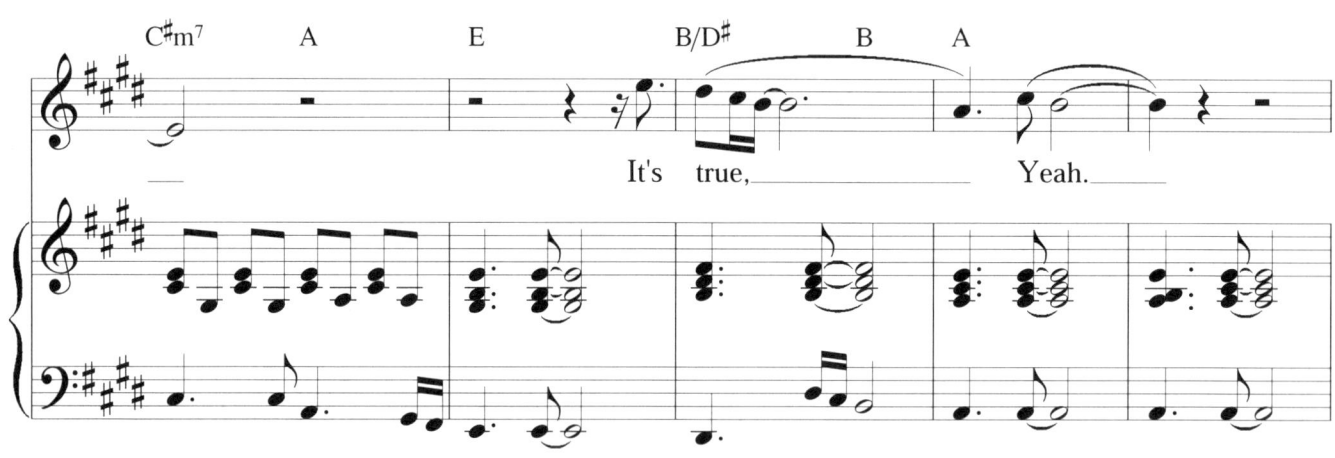

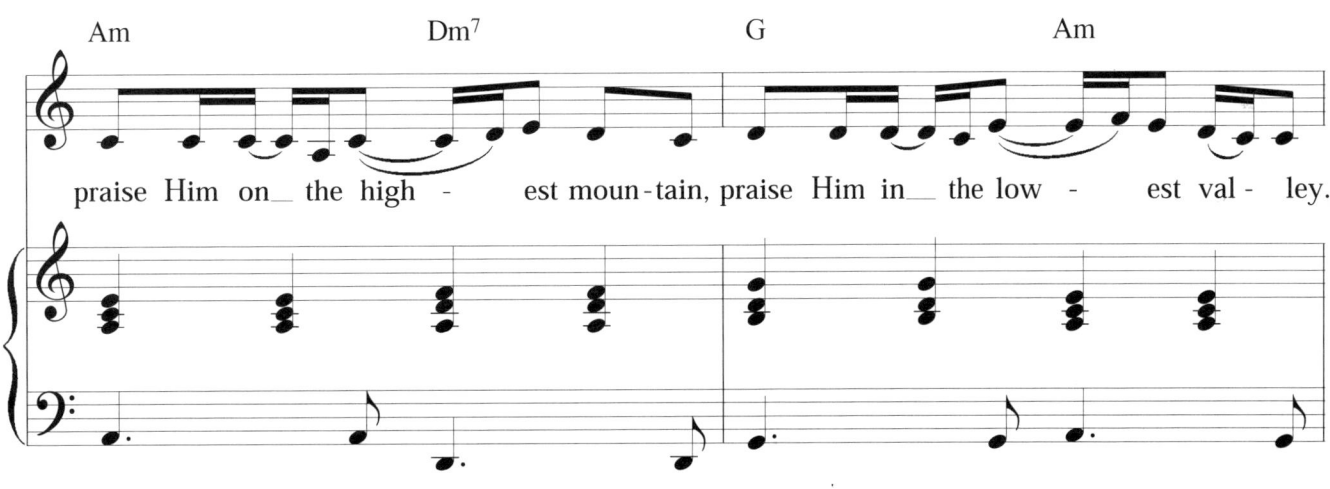

29

Getcha

Key of Am
♩=92

Words and Music by
Wayne Huirua, Libby Huirua,
and Chris de Jong

I got-ta get-cha in my life__ 'Cause on-ly You can sa-tis-fy.__ I got-ta get-cha in my life.__ There's on-ly You.__ I got-ta get-cha in my there's on-ly You__ That can make a blind man see,__ That can make__ my spi-rit free,__

From the Here to Him Music release: "Love" (Parachute Band)
© 1999 Parachute Music, Admin. in the U.S. and Canada by Howard Publishing, Inc., West Monroe, LA (BMI)
www.worshipextreme.com

That can do the things You do,___ There's on-ly You.___ That can make a bet-ter way,___

That can make a bright-er day,___ That can do the things You do,___ There's on-ly You.___

I got-ta get-cha in my There's on-ly You.___

You're the One, You're the One that I live for. Ev'-ry day I live my life I wan-na get more

C/G   **D⁹/F#**

Of You, of You, of You and Your sweet love.

Am

You're the One, you're the One that I cry for,

E(#5)/G#

'Cause in me You saw some-one that You could die for,

C/G   **D⁹/F#**   **Am**

My Lord, my Love, Hear me say, I got-ta get-cha in my

Give It Up

Key of Em

♩=110

Words and Music by
Wayne and Libby Huirua

Come in-to this place where the Lord re-sides, come on let's praise Him.

Come in-to this place, lift His name on high, come on let's praise Him.

He's a God of glo-ry, a God of grace, a God of mer-cy so

From the Here to Him Music release: "Adore" (Parachute Band)
© 1998 Parachute Music, Admin. in the U.S. and Canada by Howard Publishing, Inc., West Monroe, LA (BMI)
www.worshipextreme.com

1. B7♯5 B♯2/D♯ Em7 B♯2/D♯ Em7
2. Baug7
wor - thy of our praise. Come on let's praise Him.
wor - thy of our praise.
Em7 A13 G13 A13 Em7
He is the Lord, there's no doubt, so let's shout it out for Je - sus.
Em7 A13 G13 A13 Baug7
He is our Sa - vior, He made ya, cre - a - ted for His plea - sure.
B2/D♯ 1. Em7 B2/D♯ Em7 2. B2/D♯ Em7
Give it up, give it all to Je - sus, Praise Him.
Him

Glorify

Key of G
♩=107

Words and Music by
Dean Rush

Glo - ri - fy, You light up my way.

Sanc - ti - fy, My life, washed in Your grace. Your love for me, Dis - played o - pen - ly.

From the Here to Him Music release: "Journey Closer" (Form)
© 1999 Parachute Music, Admin. in the U.S. and Canada by Howard Publishing, Inc., West Monroe, LA (BMI)
www.worshipextreme.com

Yeah. All I want is You.

My heart, it burns for You. There's no one

else like You. All I want is You.

My heart, it burns for You.

39

God of Glory

Key of Bm

♩=65

Words and Music by
Wayne and Libby Huirua

In Your pre-sence there is joy,_ in Your pre-sence there is free-dom,_ but the great-est joy of all_ is to know we've made You smile._ In Your pre-sence there_ is life, in Your pre-sence there_ is hea-ling,_ but the great-est joy of all_ is to know we've reached Your heart._

From the Here to Him Music release: "Adore" (Parachute Band)
© 1998 Parachute Music, Admin. in the U.S. and Canada by Howard Publishing, Inc., West Monroe, LA (BMI)
www.worshipextreme.com

God of glo-ry we give You praise, Lift You up in this ho-ly place. Our hearts are rea-dy, our lives made new. It's all we long to do. God of glo-ry, we give You praise. We lift You up in this ho-ly place. Our hearts are rea-dy our lives made new. God of glo-ry we wor-ship

42

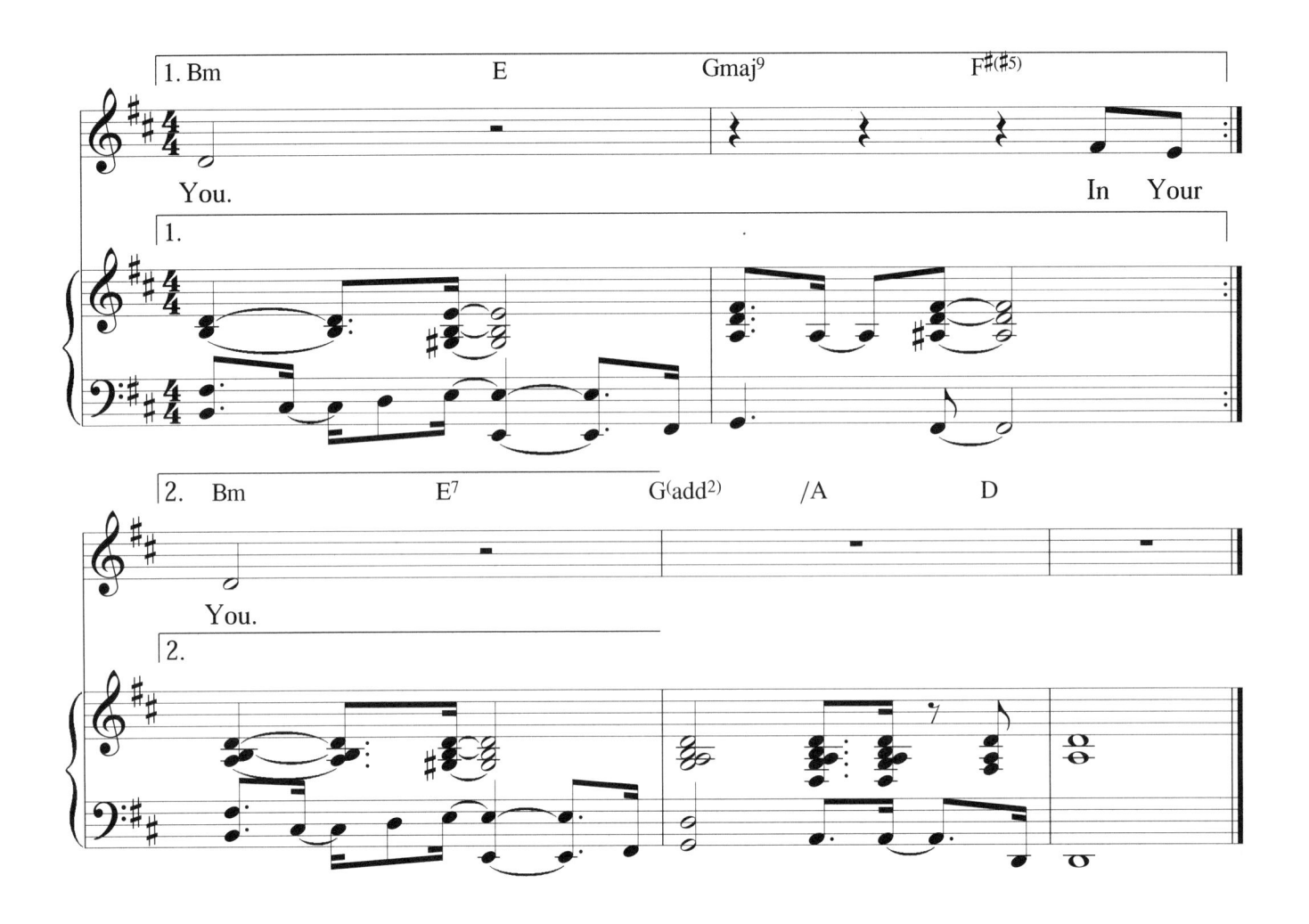

Got the Need

Key of Gm
♩=133

Words and Music by
Wayne and Libby Huirua

Je - sus,___ You__ have claimed my_ soul.___

Je - sus,___ You__ have_ made_ me_ whole.___ Ear - ly in the mor - ning till late at night_ I'll love You, Lord. You're on my_ mind.___

From the Here to Him Music release: "Always and Forever" (Parachute Band)
© 1998 Parachute Music, Admin. in the U.S. and Canada by Howard Publishing, Inc., West Monroe, LA (BMI)
www.worshipextreme.com

Gi - ven me life from up a - bove____ and I can't get e - nough____ of Your love. I got the need____ to let You know.____ I be - lieve it, and I feel it, and I got to let it show.____ I got the need

B♭maj7/C
B♭6/C
B♭maj7/C
Gm7
to let You know.
E♭6(9)
Cdim/D
3
'Cause I can't think of a bet - ter way to say,
Gm7
"I love You."
D7(6)

Key of D
♩=98

Ha Hei Beach

Words by Julian Currin
Music by Dean Rush

From the Here to Him Music release: "Journey Closer"(Form)

www.worshipextreme.com

D D/A Em D/F♯ G
Fa - ther, Cre - a - tor, Re - veal Your - self in sol - i - tude.
A7sus4 G A
I will be Your ser - vant. I won't turn
Bm G D
a - way. I will bow
A G A
my knee. I won't be a - fraid.

Holy Anointed One

Key of D
♩=89

Words and Music by
Jason Harrison and Darin Sasser

My mouth is filled with Your prais - es, Lord. You are the rea - son we sing. You are the rea - son we come. As I en - ter in to Your pre - sence My hands are trem - bl - ing. You are the rea - son we sing. You are the rea - son we come.

From the Here to Him Music release: "Among Thorns" (Among Thorns)
© 1998 ShadowRock Publishing Group, Admin. in the U.S. and Canada by Howard Publishing, Inc., West Monroe, LA (BMI)
www.worshipextreme.com

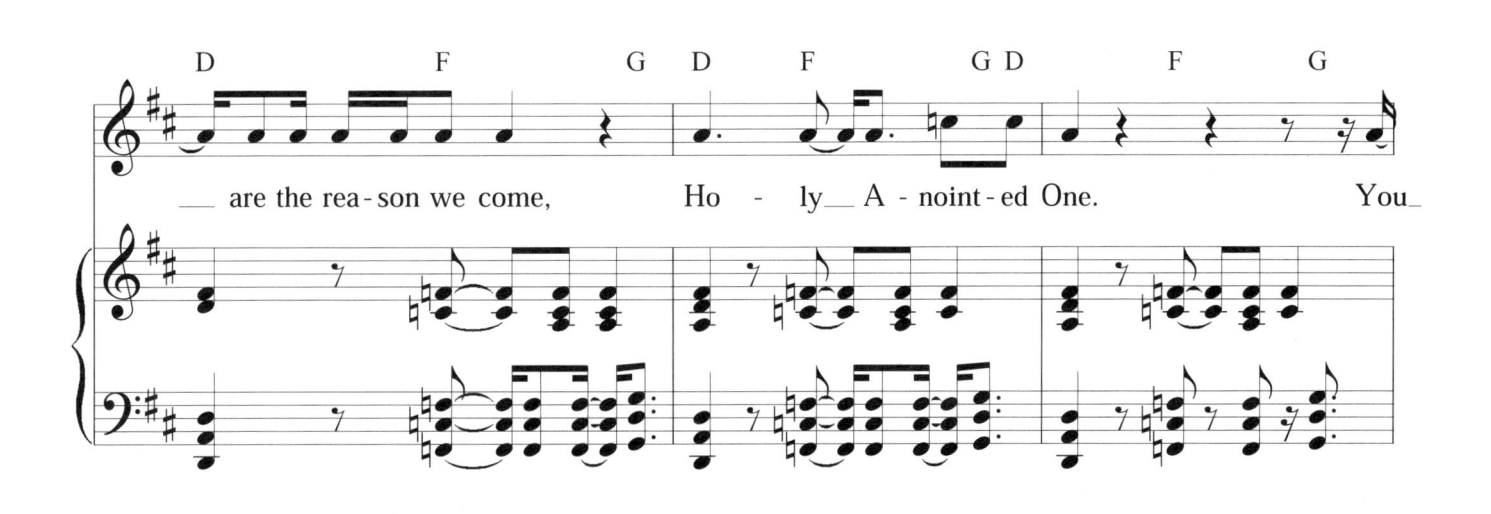

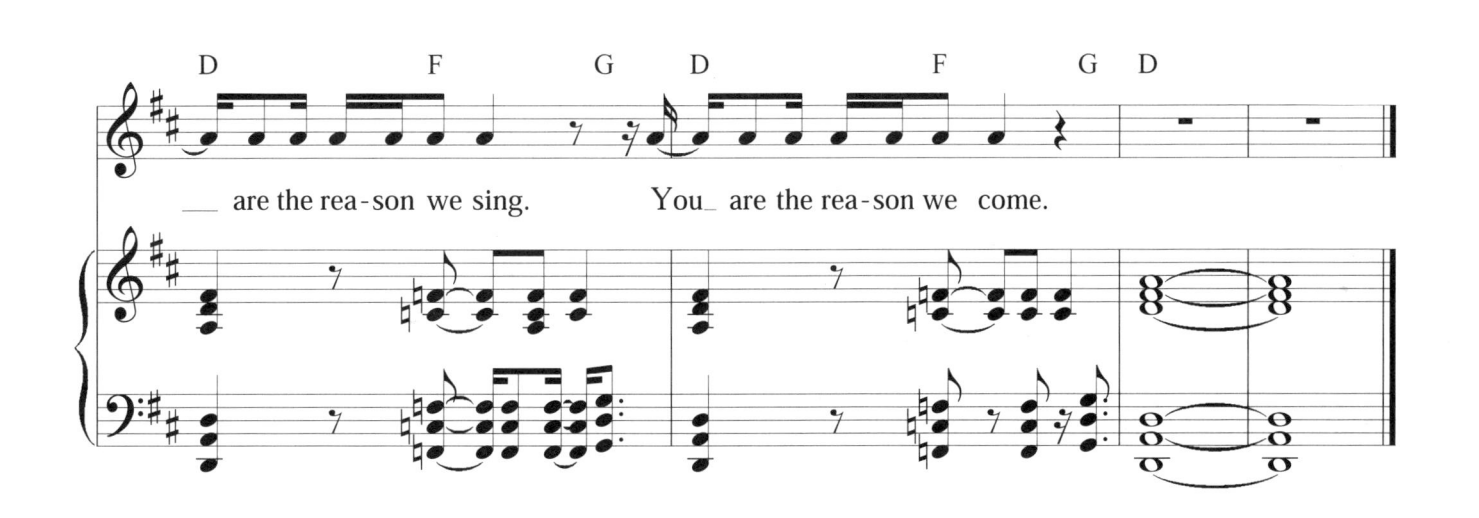

Ho - ly_ A - noint - ed One, You_ are the rea - son we sing. You_ are the rea - son we come, Ho - ly_ A - noint - ed One. You_ are the rea - son we sing. You_ are the rea - son we come.

Holy One

Key of E
♩=110

Words and Music by
Andrew Ulugia

Holy One, Righteous King,
Merciful You are, Merciful I'll be.
Broken One, Bruised for me,
In Your death, Oh Lord, You have set me free. Be-cause

From the Here to Him Music release: "Adore"(Parachute Band)
© 1998 Parachute Music, Admin. in the U.S. and Canada by Howard Publishing, Inc., West Monroe, LA (BMI)
www.worshipextreme.com

| B/D# | A/C# | E Esus⁴ E |

Your Fa - ther loved me so You came

| B/D# | A/C# | G#/B# G# |

to me, Lord Je - sus so that I would know

| C#m | A | B/A | G#m |

Love un - con - di - tion - al And life e - ter - nal.

| A(add2) E/G# | F#m E | D A/C# |

Oh my Lord, my God, my

1. Bsus4 B
2. B
E F#m B/D#
all.
all.
Ri - sen One,
1.
2.
E F#m B/D# E F#m B/D#
Ma - jes - ty,
Res - to - ra -
E A/C# A B E
- tion come, breathe new life in me.

Holy Spirit

Key of E
♩=103

Words and Music by
Jason Harrison and Darin Sasser

Ho - ly Spi - rit, take con - trol. Fan the flames with - in my soul.

2nd x to CODA

Ho - ly Spi - rit, take con - trol.

Breathe down deep with - in my spi - rit.

Strong Fire burn.

From the Here to Him Music release: "Among Thorns"(Among Thorns)
© 1998 ShadowRock Publishing Group, Admin. in the U.S. and Canada by Howard Publishing, Inc., West Monroe, LA (BMI)
www.worshipextreme.com

How I Long for You

Key of G

♩=67

Words and Music by
Jamie Burgess

Lord, how I long for You. And Lord, how I long to wor-ship You In Your holy place, Standing face to face, My Father, How I long for You.

From the Here to Him Music release: "Always and Forever" (Parachute Band)
© 1998 Parachute Music, Admin. in the U.S. and Canada by Howard Publishing, Inc., West Monroe, LA (BMI)
www.worshipextreme.com

(You,) How I long for You.

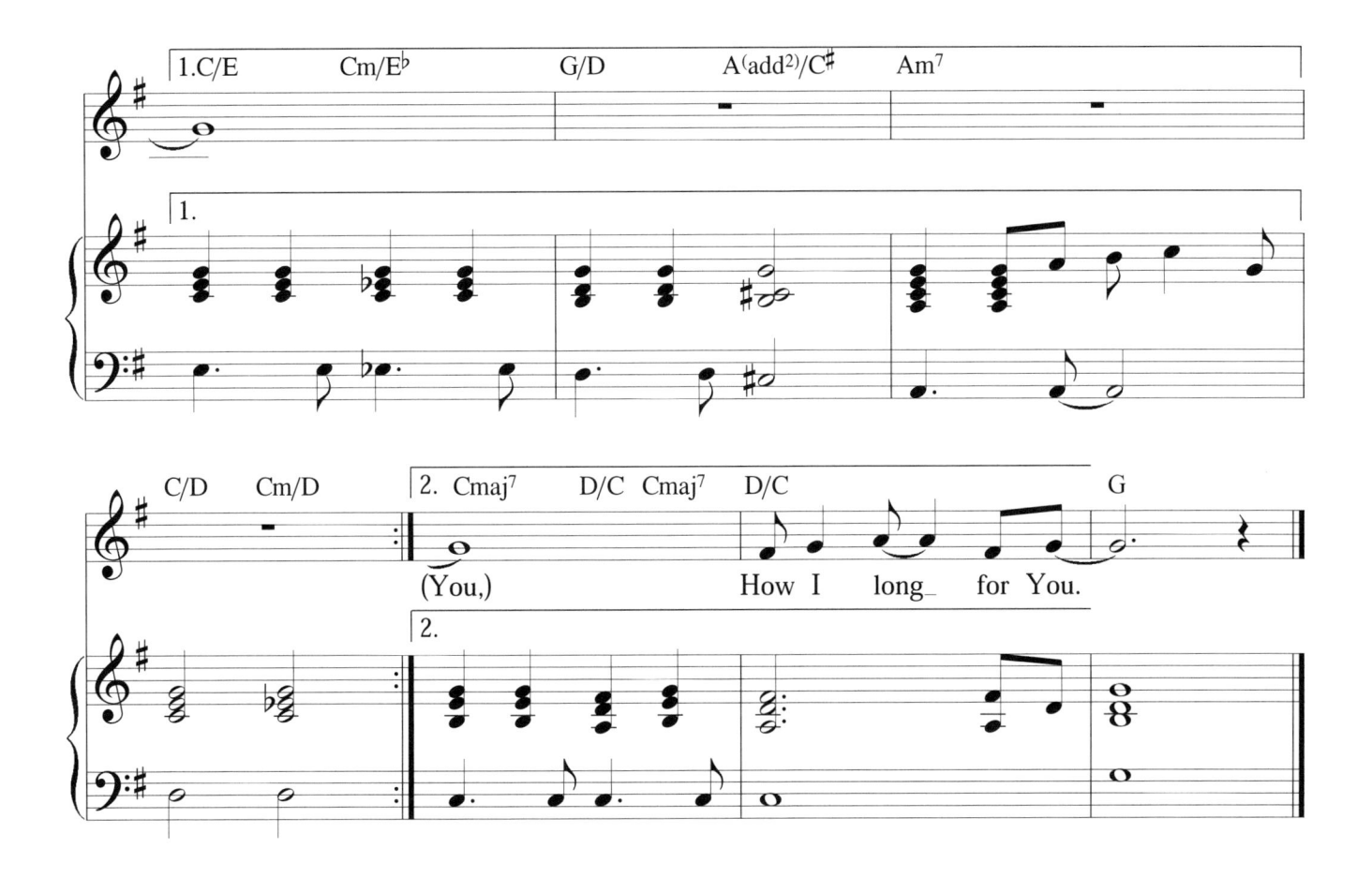

55

Hungry For You

Key of Bb

Words and Music by
Bonnie Low

I'm hungry for You, so hungry for You. I'm hungry for You, so hungry for You. Needing your touch, just the touch of Your hand.

From the Here to Him Music release: "You Alone" (Parachute Band)
© 1997 Parachute Music, Admin. in the U.S. and Canada by Howard Publishing, Inc., West Monroe, LA (BMI)
www.worshipextreme.com

Show'r down Your sweet, sweet rain on my thirsty land. I'm hungry for You, so hungry for You. I'm hungry for You, So hungry for You.

I am Aware

Key of Eb
♩=99

Words and Music by
Sarah McBride

Oh, the one who is for-giv-en much is a-ware of the po-wer of His love. And the one who had been set free is a-ware of the pa-tience in His love. The one who has found joy is a-ware of the good-ness of God.

From the Here to Him Music release: "Always and Forever" (Parachute Band)
© 1998 Parachute Music, Admin. in the U.S. and Canada by Howard Publishing, Inc., West Monroe, LA (BMI)
www.worshipextreme.com

And the one who calls out His name never will be the same. I am aware of the goodness of God. I will hold on to the promise He made. I am aware. I'm forgiven and whole through the power of the cross and His love.

I am aware of the power of God. He is the one who is in control. I will have faith, faith in His love. Cause His truth is everlasting to the very end. (Oh, the)

I Fall Down

Key of A
♩=90

Words and Music by
Shonelle Barnes

I see You, Lord in the most holy place.

Where angels tremble and lay down in worship.

I stand in wonder, longing to draw near.

You catch my eye and call me in.

From the Here to Him Music release: "Always and Forever" (Parachute Band)
© 1998 Parachute Music, Admin. in the U.S. and Canada by Howard Publishing, Inc., West Monroe, LA (BMI)
www.worshipextreme.com

D(add2)
A E
F♯m D
A E
I fall down
in awe of You.
F♯m D
A E
I fall down
F♯m D
A E
F♯m D
in awe of You.

I Lift Up Your Name

Key of F

Words and Music by
Jason Harrison and Darrin Sasser

With ev-'ry breath that I take,_ ev-'ry sound that I make, I lift up Your name._

With ev-'ry thing that's with-in,_ ev-'ry-where that You send_

_ me, I lift up Your name._ Ho-ly Spi-rit, You lead_

_ me, Spi-rit, You fill_ me with Your gen-tle ways.

From the Here to Him Music release: AWE (Alternative Worship Experience)
© 2000 ShadowRock Publishing Group, Admin. in the U.S. and Canada by Howard Publishing, Inc., West Monroe, LA
www.worshipextreme.com

Ho - ly Spi - rit, You fill___ me, Spi - rit, You fill___ me with Your gen - tle ways._ May my heart_ be_ deep - er than the songs I sing._ May my love_ flow_ strong - er than a riv - er. I'll praise You 'til Your king - dom comes.

Key of Ab

I Stand In Awe

Words and Music by
Louis Collins

From the Here to Him Music release: "Love" (Parachute Band)

www.worshipextreme.com

head in rev - er - ence to You, Migh - ty God. I will pro -
claim how won - der - ful and mar - ve - lous You are. I raise my
hand to You, my awe - some King. I stand in awe of You, In
awe of You, my God.

I Will Call

Key of D
♩=97

Words and Music by Jason Parish,
Darin Sasser and Jason Harrison

From the ends of the earth, I will call out to You.
From mountain peaks I cry.
With outstretched arms I embrace Your whole mercy.
As my praises kiss the sky.

From the Here to Him Music release: "Among Thorns" (Among Thorns)
© 1998 ShadowRock Publishing Group, Admin. in the U.S. and Canada by Howard Publishing, Inc., West Monroe, LA (BMI)
www.worshipextreme.com

I will call_____ out_ to You.

It's the on - ly thing_ that I__ know_ to_ do._

I will call_____ out_ to You_

When I'm cry - ing from_ the hurt_

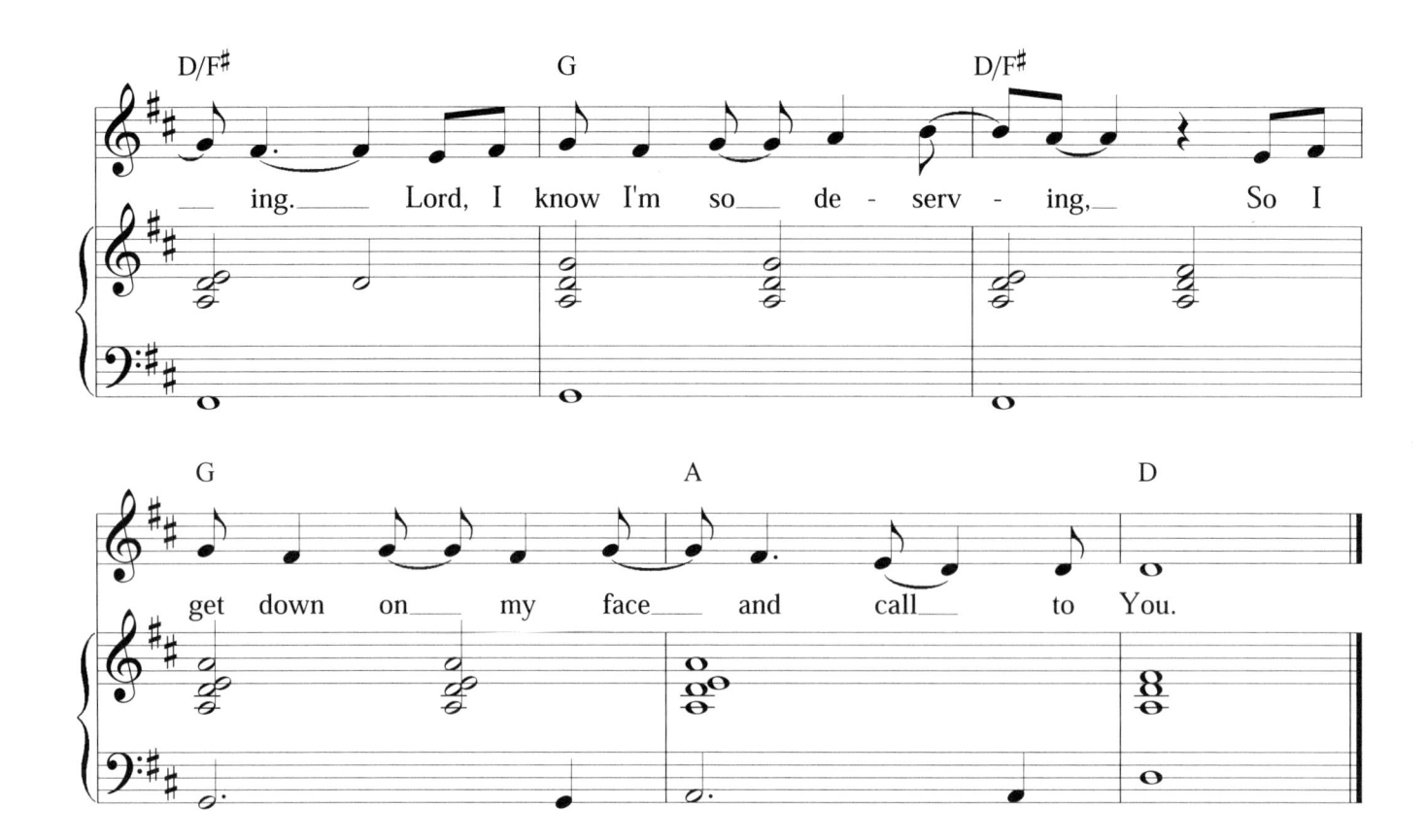

__ing. Lord, I know I'm so_ de - serv - ing,_ So I get down on_ my face_ and call_ to You.

I'm Your Servant

Key of D
♩=60

Words and Music by
Andrew Ulugia

Now in-to Your pres-ence, Lord, I will bold-ly come.

It's on-ly by Your grace, Oh Lord, It's no-thing I have done.

Grant me Your ser-vant heart that I might live like You. As You set

From the Here to Him Music release: "Always and Forever" (Parachute Band)
© 1998 Parachute Music, Admin. in the U.S. and Canada by Howard Publishing, Inc., West Monroe, LA (BMI)
www.worshipextreme.com

me a-part, I will hum-bly share the love I found in You.

I'm Your ser-vant here I am. Bend-ed knees and o-pen hands.

Lord, I hear Your voice to-day Lord I hear and I o-bey.

When I'm weak will You be strong? When I'm lost, will You lead me home?

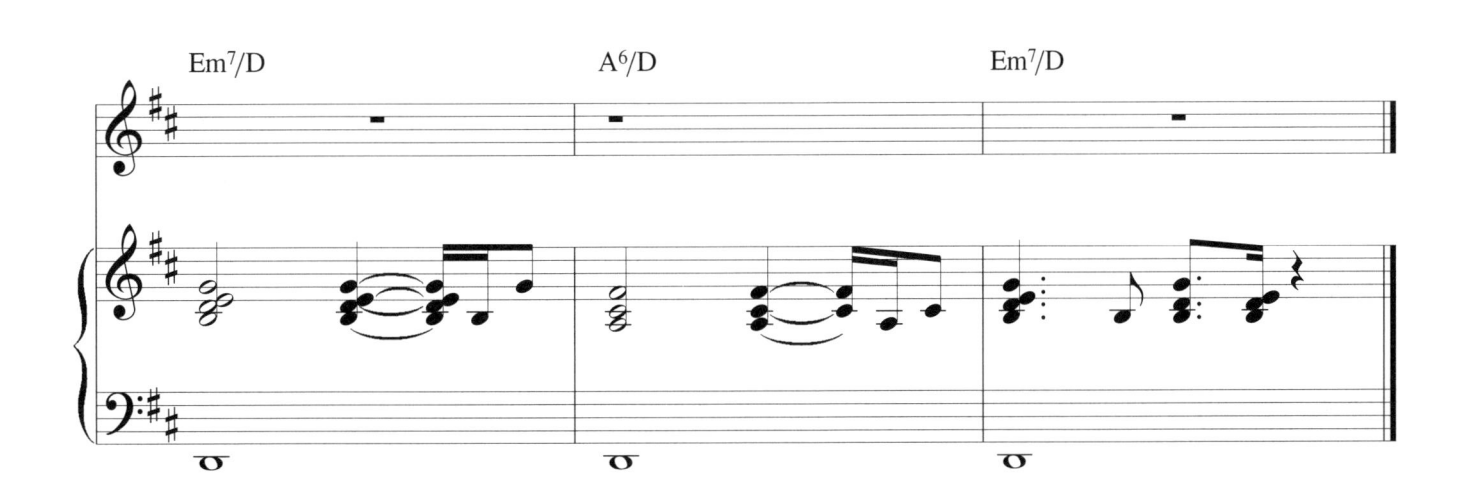

Though I strug-gle on the way, Would You use me an-y way?

Lord, I give my self to-day.

Immerse Me

Key of D
♩=69

Words by Dean Rush
Music by Dean Rush
and Justion Pilbrow

Im - merse me in Your love, Im - merse me. Ho - ly I be-
come, You heal me. A - dopt - ed, I be - long, I'm cho - sen.
Paid for by Your Son, bro - ken. Im - merse me in Your love,
im - merse me. Ho - ly I be - come, You heal me.

From the Here to Him Music release: "Journey Closer" (Form)
© 1999 Parachute Music, Admin. in the U.S. and Canada by Howard Publishing, Inc., West Monroe, LA (BMI)
www.worshipextreme.com

D
Asus4/C#
Bm7
You heal me.
A
G
D/F#
Yeah,
Yeah,
G
Bm7
A/C#
D
You heal me,
Asus4/C#
Bm7
A
You heal me,
Yeah.

Lord, I come before You. Lay me down.

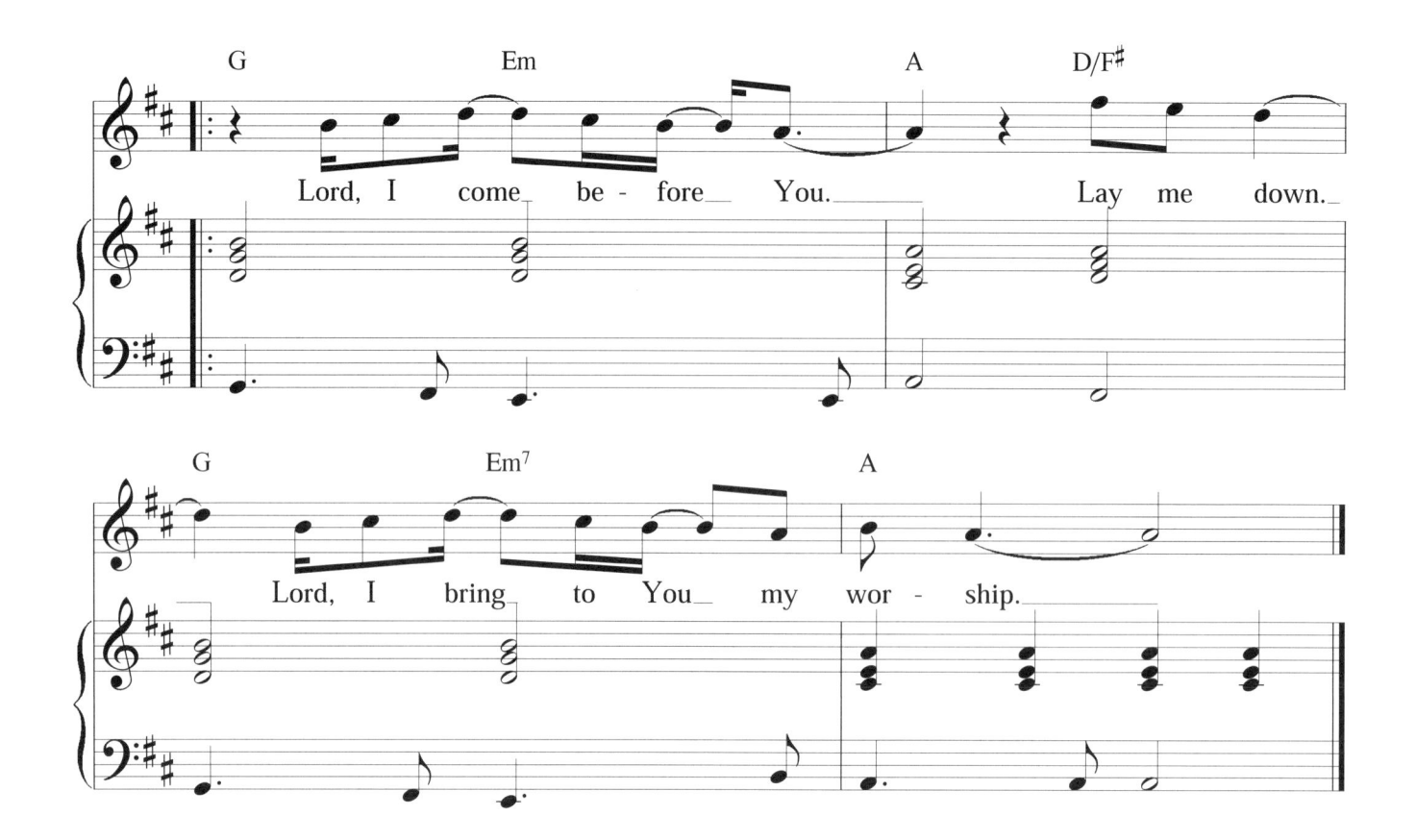

Lord, I bring to You my worship.

In The Name Of Jesus

Key of Em

Words and Music by
Wayne and Libby Huirua

Who can stand in Your pre-sence, Who dares to e-ven try?
We can stand in Your pre-sence, You've giv-en us the right,

All pow'rs and prin-ci-pal-i-ties
Co-vered by the blood of Je-sus,

1. must fall be-fore Your throne. But
   Now we can stand and fight.

2.

From the Here to Him Music release: "You Alone" (Parachute Band)
© 1997 Parachute Music, Admin. in the U.S. and Canada by Howard Publishing, Inc., West Monroe, LA (BMI)
www.worshipextreme.com

This is where we draw the line. Don't believe the devil's lies. Pow'r of God is on our side. We belong to Jesus Christ. Jesus Christ.

In the name, in the name of Jesus. In the name of Jesus Christ.

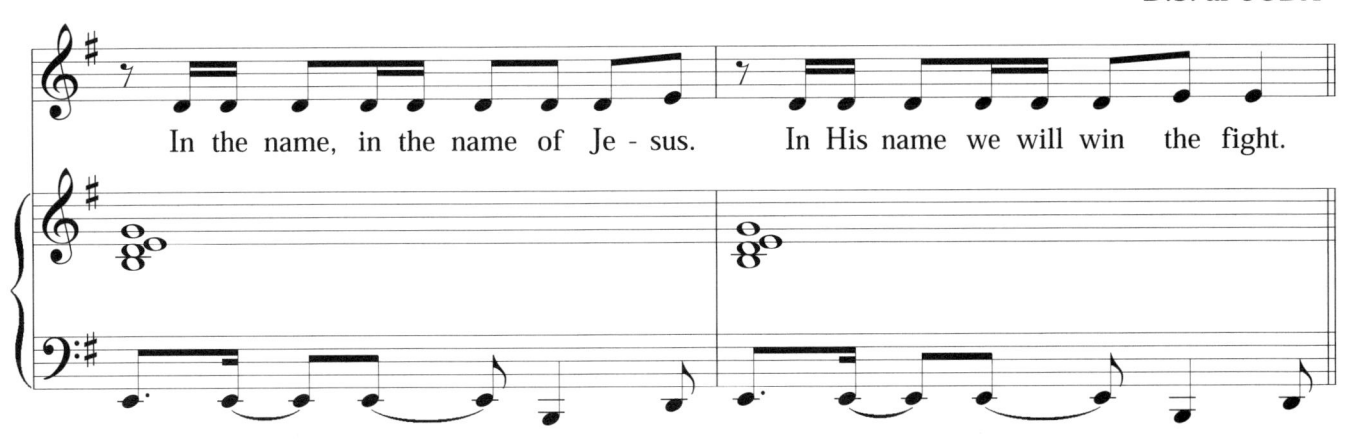

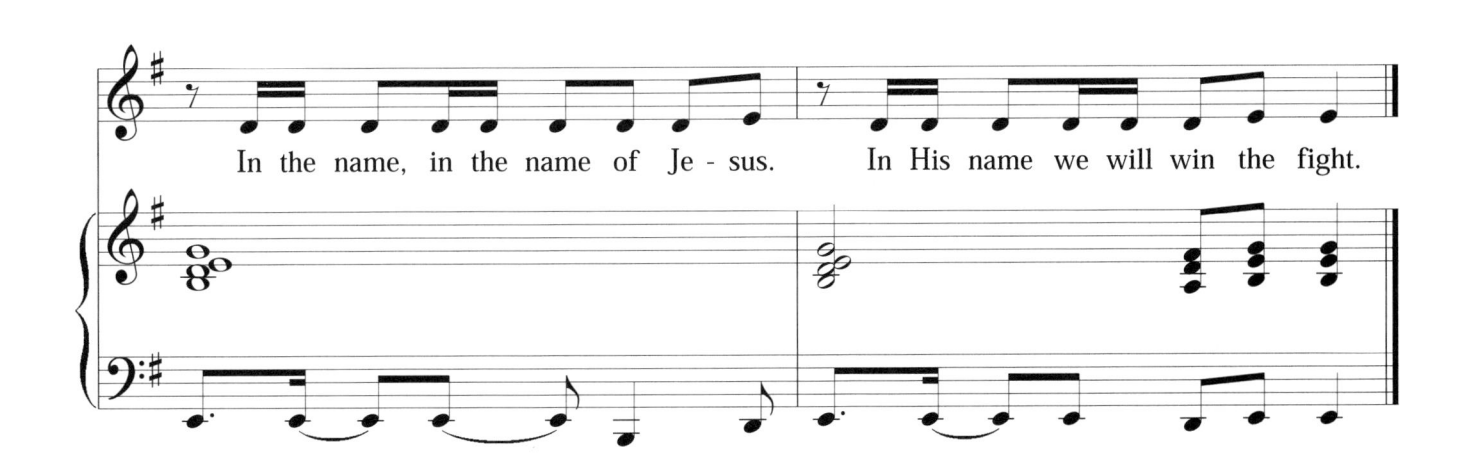

D.S. al CODA

In the name, in the name of Je-sus. In His name we will win the fight.

CODA

Em7

In the name, in the name of Je-sus. In the name of Je-sus Christ.

In the name, in the name of Je-sus. In His name we will win the fight.

Inspired

Key of F#m

Words and Music by
James Sampson

♩=100

From the Here to Him Music release: "Love"(Parachute Band)

road is long and though we stum-ble, We hear Your voice and we know Your hand.

Guide us, Lord, Keep us hum-ble.

Hear us, Lord, this we pray In- In- spired.

81

Jesus

Key of F

Words and Music by
Richard Knott

So near to me, I can feel Your touch. So close by me, A whisper is enough. Love and kindness overflow my soul. New songs ex-

From the Here to Him Music release: "Love" (Parachute Band)
© 1999 Parachute Music, Admin. in the U.S. and Canada by Howard Publishing, Inc., West Monroe, LA (BMI)
www.worshipextreme.com

pres-sing your love, a-ma-zing love. You're the air that I breathe,

You're the rea-son I sing, My Je-sus, Je-sus.

You're the one I a-dore, Oh my spi-rit, it soars, My Je-

1. -sus, Je-sus.

2. -sus, Je-sus.

Jesus, I Bow Down

Key of A

Words and Music by
Andrew Ulugia

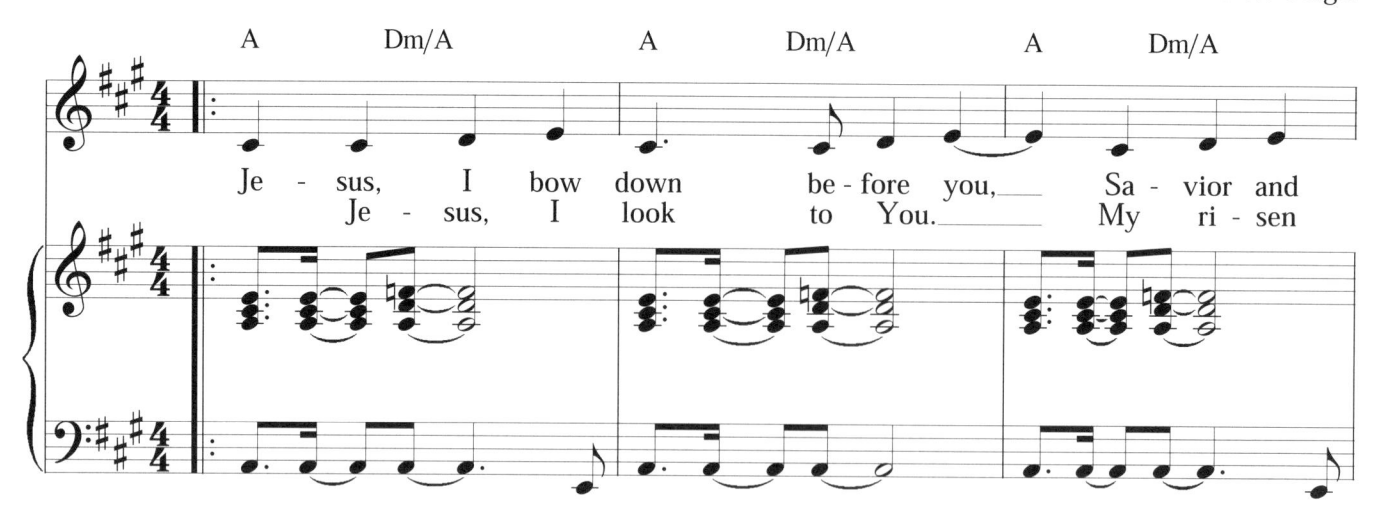

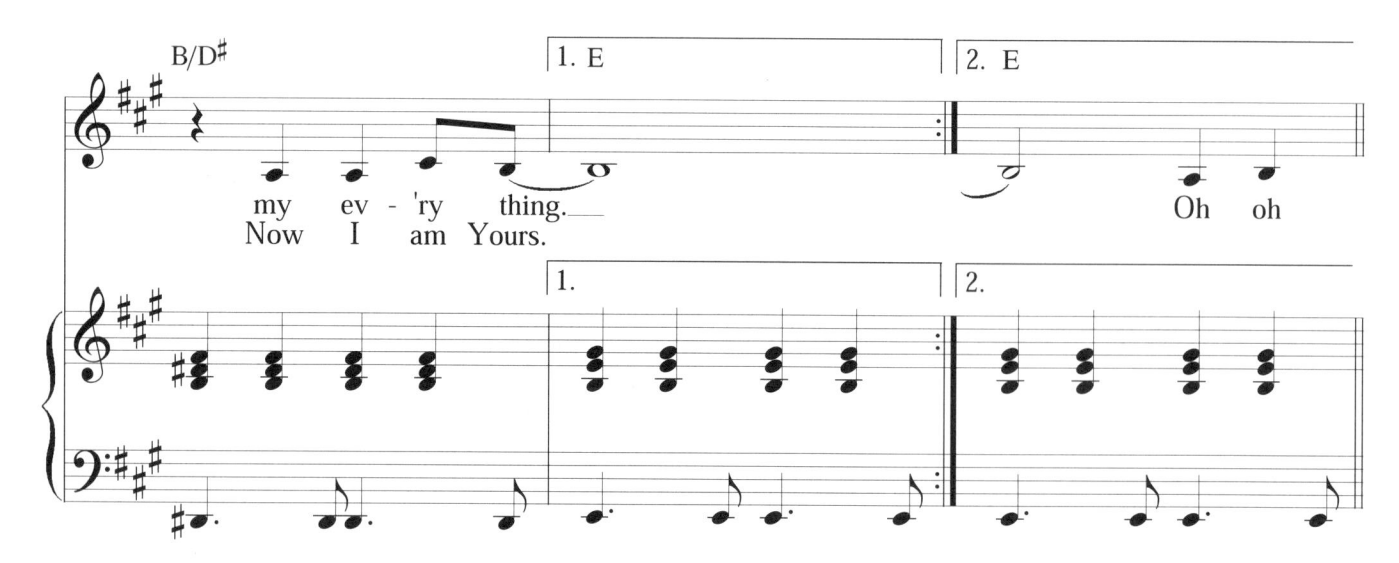

Je - sus, I bow down be - fore you, Sa - vior and King.
Je - sus, I look to You. My ri - sen Lord.

There is no o - ther love, my ev - 'ry thing.
Your love has res - cued me, Now I am Yours.

Oh oh

From the Here to Him Music release: "You Alone" (Parachute Band)
© 1997 Parachute Music, Admin. in the U.S. and Canada by Howard Publishing, Inc., West Monroe, LA (BMI)
www.worshipextreme.com

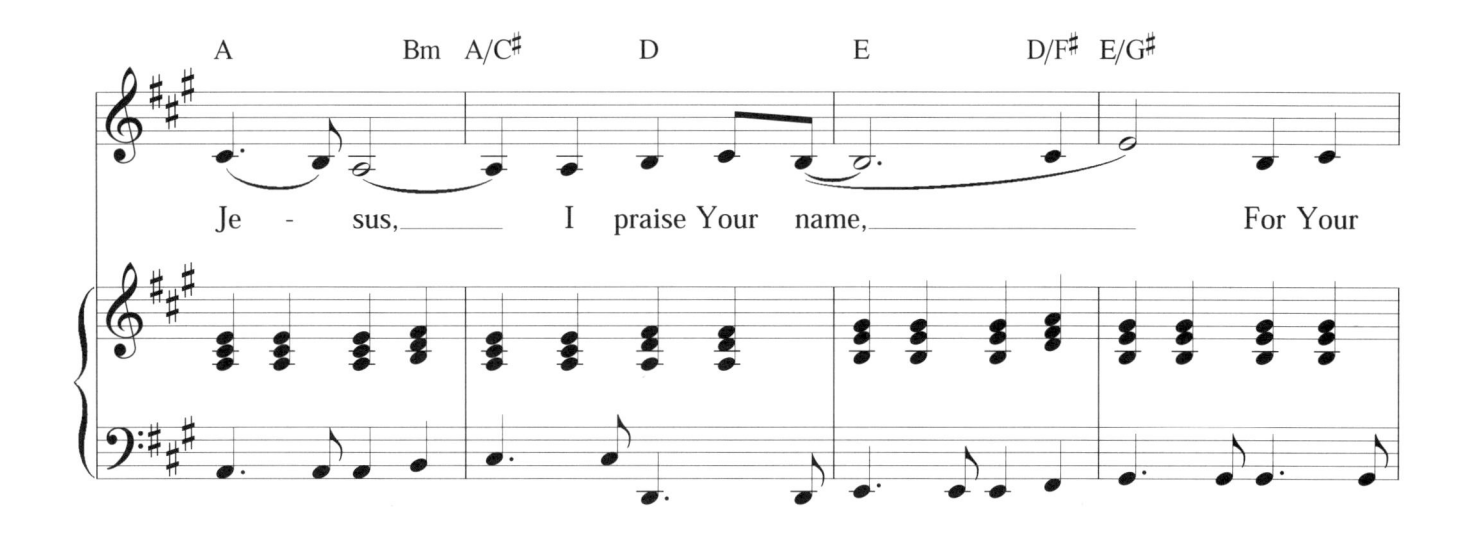

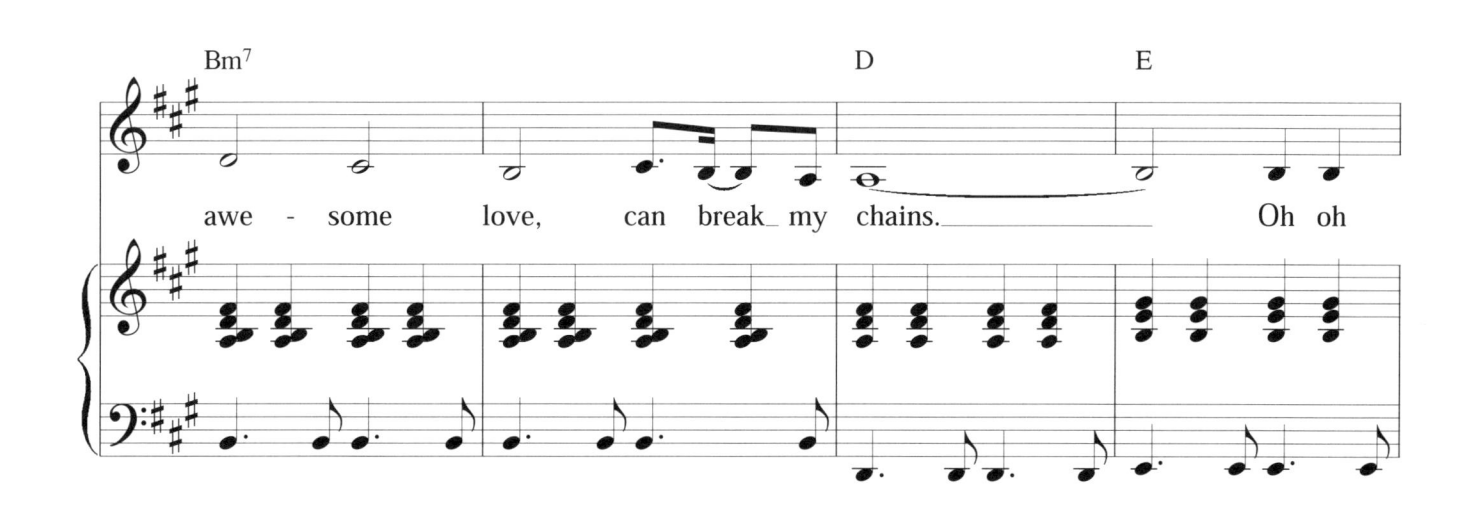

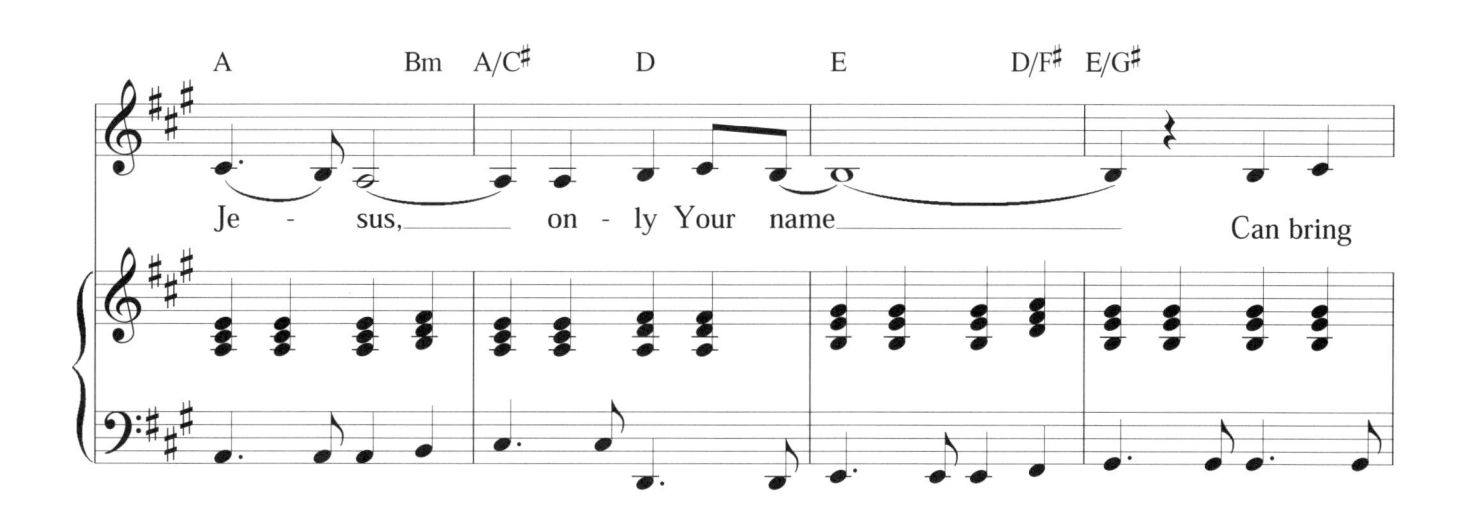

| A | Bm A/C# | D E | D/F# E/G# |

Je - sus, _____ I praise Your name, _____ For Your

Bm⁷ | | D | E |

awe - some love, can break my chains. _____ Oh oh

| A | Bm A/C# | D E | D/F# E/G# |

Je - sus, _____ on - ly Your name _____ Can bring

li - ber - ty. Je - sus, You set me free to - day.

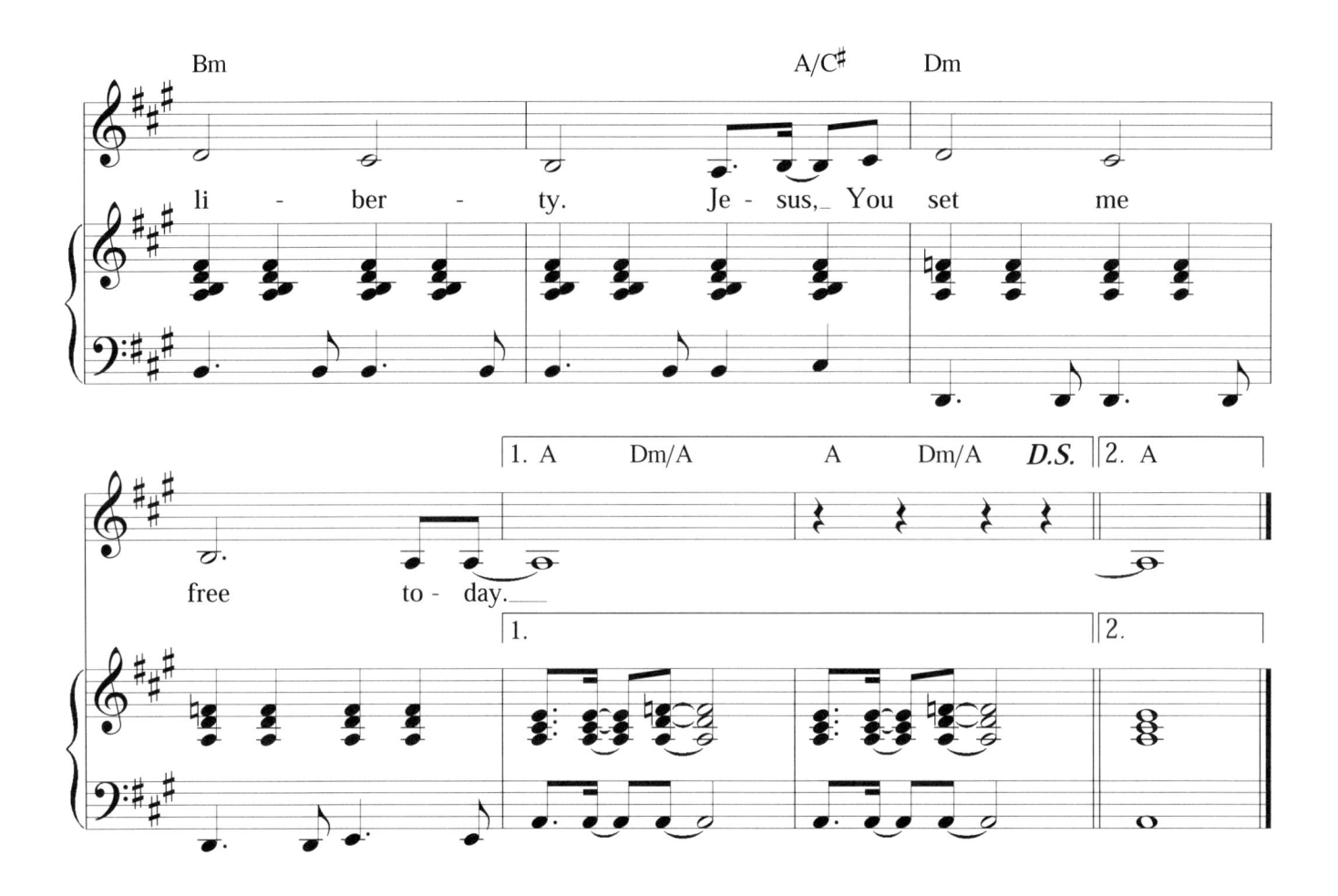

Jesus Is Real

Key of C

Words and Music by
Phillip Fuemana

Je- sus is real. The love I feel.

Je- sus is real. The love I feel.

Last X to CODA

When you walk through the val-ley of sha-dows, When you walk through the val-ley of fear, When you

From the Here to Him Music release: "You Alone" (Parachute Band)
© 1997 Parachute Music, Admin. in the U.S. and Canada by Howard Publishing, Inc., West Monroe, LA (BMI)
www.worshipextreme.com

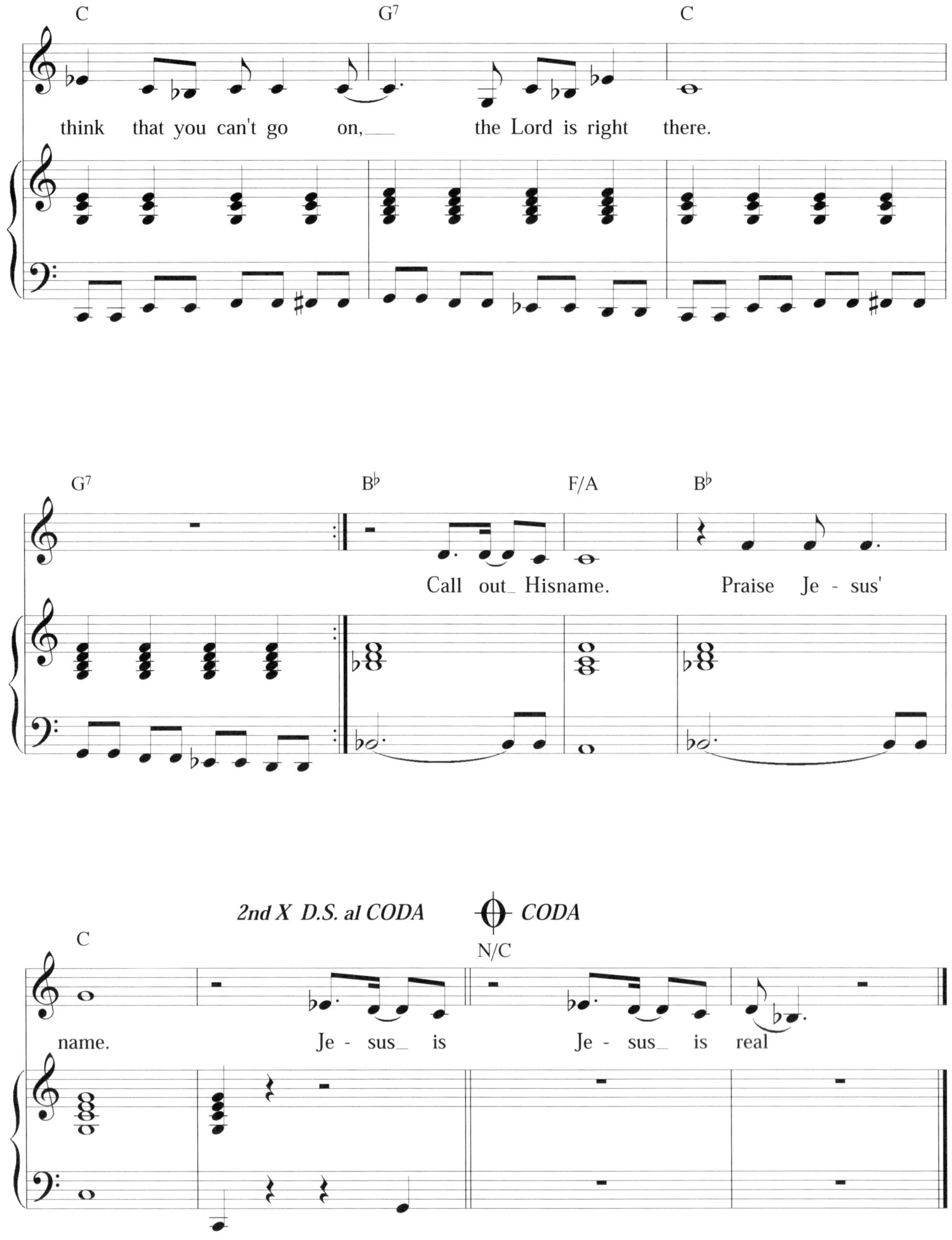
C G7 C
think that you can't go on,___ the Lord is right there.
G7 B♭ F/A B♭
Call out_ Hisname. Praise Je - sus'
2nd X D.S. al CODA
CODA
C N/C
name. Je - sus_ is Je - sus_ is real

Key of G

Journey Closer

Words and Music by
Dean Rush

♩=99

From the Here to Him Music release: "Journey Closer" (Form)

G/B D/F♯
1. D C D
go from You?
1.
C
2. D C
My hand stretched out,
2.
D C D G
Your life You laid down.
You are strong,

your love never ends. Though I fall,

You save me again. You are strong,

Your love never ends.

Though I fall, You save me again.

Let Everything

Key of E
♩=112

Words and Music by
Bruce Conlon

I will praise You, oh Lord a-mong the na-tions now. I will sing of You A-mong all the peo-ples. For great is Your love, High-er than the hea-vens. Your

From the Here to Him Music release: "Journey Closer" (Form)
© 1999 Parachute Music, Admin. in the U.S. and Canada by Howard Publishing, Inc., West Monroe, LA (BMI)
www.worshipextreme.com

faith - ful - ness___ Reach - es__ the sky.__

Be ex - alt - ed, oh God_

High a - bove__ the hea - vens._____ And let Your

glo - ry_ be o - ver the earth,_ High a - bove_ the hea

94

Let God Arise

Key: E

Words and Music by
SCOTT REED

In four ♩ = 114

Copyright © 2000 BetterThanNew Music
P.O. Box 681046 Franklin, TN 37068-1046.
All Rights Reserved. Used by Permission. International Copyright Secured.

I live
I walk
I move
I breathe
I have a firm foun-da-tion in You
I seek to know Your pow-er in me
So as we wait on You
In fear and awe Oh Lord
Re-veal Your face to us
And with one voice we will cry out
Let God A-rise

Cues: Opt. harmony

Chorus
17
E A C♯m7 Bsus E A
f
Let God A - rise
20
C♯m7 Bsus E A C♯m7 Bsus
Last time to Coda
Un - veil our eyes
Let God A - rise
23
1. E A C♯m7 Bsus
2. E A C♯m7 Bsus
D.S. (to Verse)
or go to Bridge
Let God A - rise
Bridge
27
A2
mp Cued harmony on repeats
C♯m7
One voice one song we cry to You
With hearts with hands
mp gradually build on repeats

30
A2
we worship You This day this place we come into
33
C♯m7
1. 2. 3.
4.
Your house Your throne we rev-'rence You we rev-'rence You
D.S. al Coda (to Chorus)
36
F♯m7
E2/G♯
A2
Cues: Opt. harmony
Bsus
f
Let God A-rise
CODA
40
E
A
C♯m7
Bsus
E
rit.

Let Your Glory Fall

Key of F

♩=65

Words and Music by
Paul Zaia

I bow my knee, with each beat of my heart I worship You. Lord, to know You more to stand here and adore the glory of Your presence. Your righteousness, The beauty of Your holiness. Let Your

From the Here to Him Music release: "Adore" (Parachute Band)
© 1998 Parachute Music, Admin. in the U.S. and Canada by Howard Publishing, Inc., West Monroe, LA (BMI)
www.worshipextreme.com

glo - ry____ fall____ Now in____ this place.

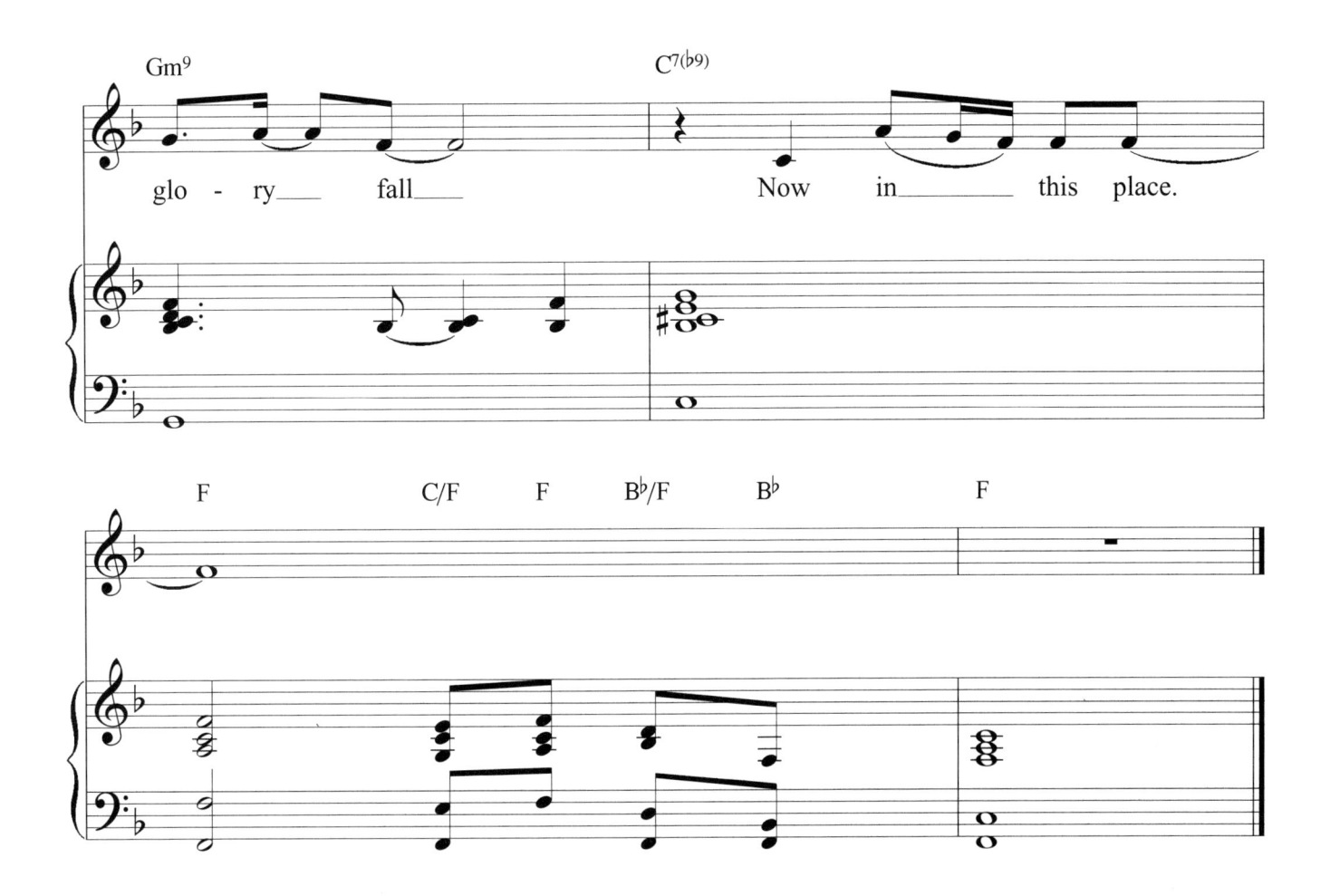

Living Fountain

Key of E
♩=137

Words and Music by
Jason and Darin Sasser

Drink the water from the Living Fountain. Taste the water from the streams of life. Cup your hands and receive the Fountain. Take a drink and relieve the dry. Open up Your floodgates. Let the King of Glory come down.

From the Here to Him Music release: "Among Thorns" (Among Thorns)
© 1998 ShadowRock Publishing Group, Admin. in the U.S. and Canada by Howard Publishing, Inc., West Monroe, LA (BMI)
www.worshipextreme.com

Once I was thirs-ty. Now streams of life a-bound.

4X

Drink the wa-ter and, Drink the wa-ter and, Drink the wa-ter and thirst no more. thirst no more. thirst no more.

Lord of the Heavens

Key of D
♩=80

Words and Music by
Shaun and Mel Griffiths

Lord of the hea - vens___ I bow_ my knee and wor - ship You._
I stand be - fore_ You___ and I am a - mazed.___
I see Your beau - ty___ dis - played in ev - 'ry - thing_ You do. For You are_

From the Here to Him Music release: "Adore"(Parachute Band)
© 1998 Parachute Music, Admin. in the U.S. and Canada by Howard Publishing, Inc., West Monroe, LA (BMI)
www.worshipextreme.com

my Saviour, Lord, and King. You are the only One for me. You are the only One that I adore. In Your Son, atonement sacrifice. Through His death redemption gives new life. And I reach out,___ re - ceive___ Your___ end - less___ love.___

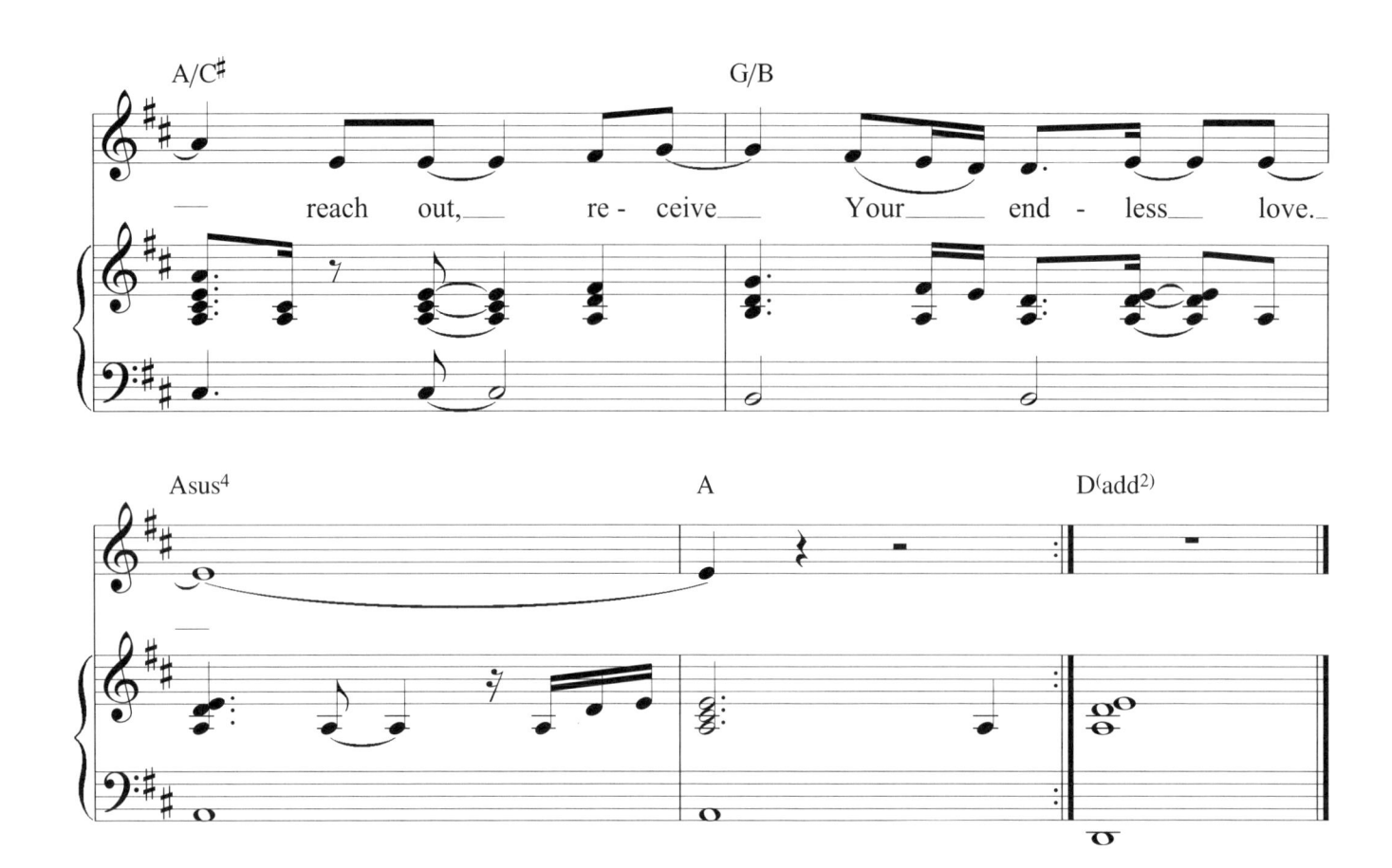

Key of F

Love Ya

words and Music by
Chris de Jong

From the Here to Him Music release: "Love"(Parachute Band)

D♭6 G♭13/E
3.
With You it's gon - na be al - right. I'm gon - na e - ver.
F9 E♭9 B♭9 D♭6
You res - cued me from the val - ley low, Heard my cry, You told
E♭7 F9 E♭9 B♭7
me so. You set my feet up - on high - er ground.
D♭6 G♭13/E
I'm do - ing fine now that You're a - round. I'm gon - na

Love You More

Key of Em
Slow Swing
♩=61

Words and Music by
Wayne Huirua

My de-light, My pre-cious one. My one de-sire Is to know Your heart and love You more. Lord, I nev-er re-a-lized to my sur-prise just how much You love me. You nev-er ev-er leave my side, for-ev-er

From the Here to Him Music release: "Always and Forever"(Parachute Band)
© 1998 Parachute Music, Admin. in the U.S. and Canada by Howard Publishing, Inc., West Monroe, LA (BMI)
www.worshipextreme.com

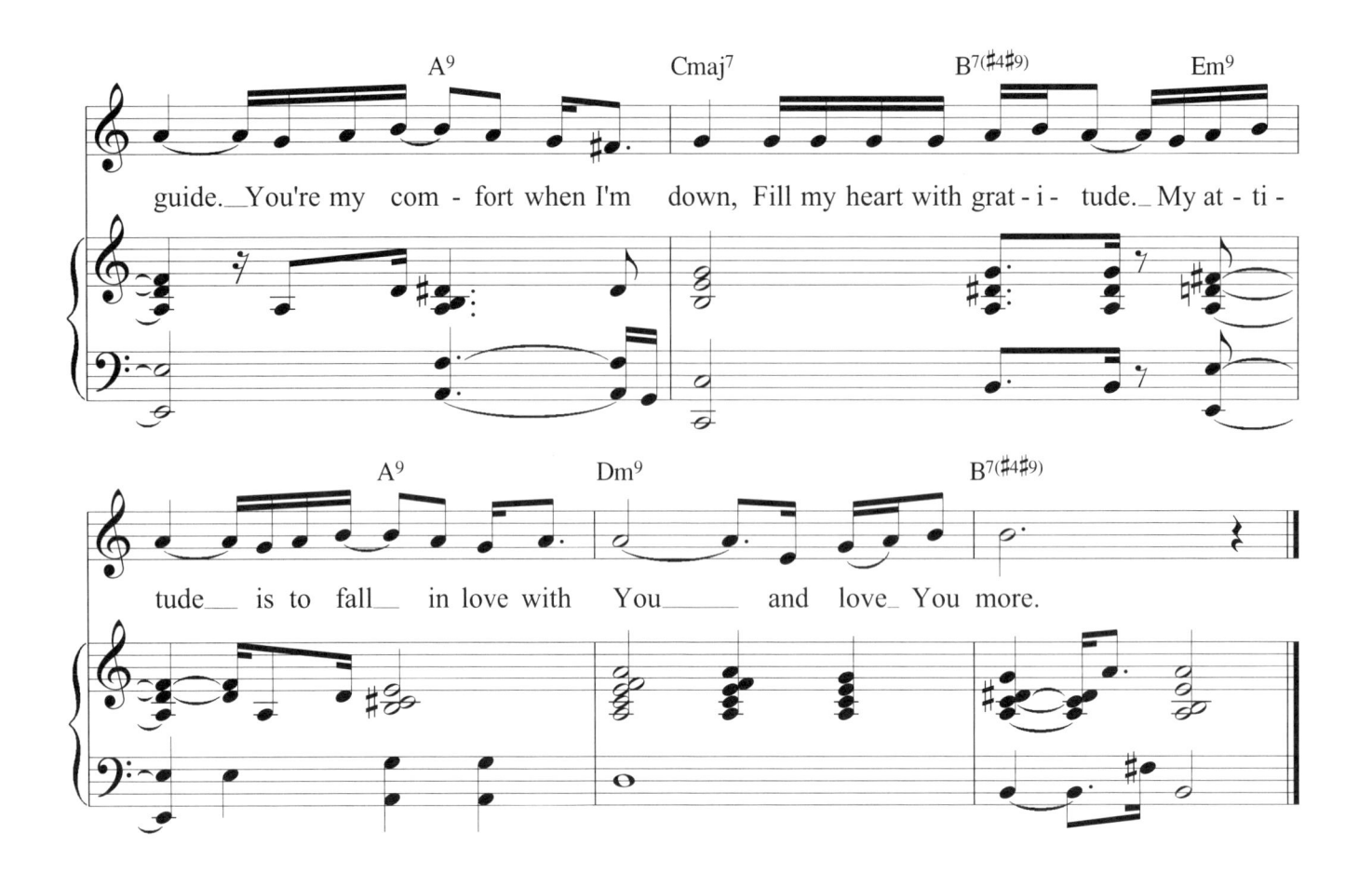

guide. You're my com-fort when I'm down, Fill my heart with grat-i-tude. My at-ti-tude is to fall in love with You and love You more.

Please Walk Beside Me

Key of C
♩=60

Words and Music by
Wayne Huirua

I of-fer up my heart to You, my Lord. On-ly in Your arms I'm safe I'm home. In You I will a-bide for-e-ver-more. You're faith-ful and You're true. Your love will see me through There's no one else but You I'll cling to. Please walk be-side me ev-'ry day

From the Here to Him Music release: "Adore" (Parachute Band)
© 1998 Parachute Music, Admin. in the U.S. and Canada by Howard Publishing, Inc., West Monroe, LA (BMI)
www.worshipextreme.com

Hold me and guide me all of the way. You give me life and destiny. Only in You can I be made free.

Last X to CODA

Today I offer up my heart completely, Lord, not just in part. Take

110

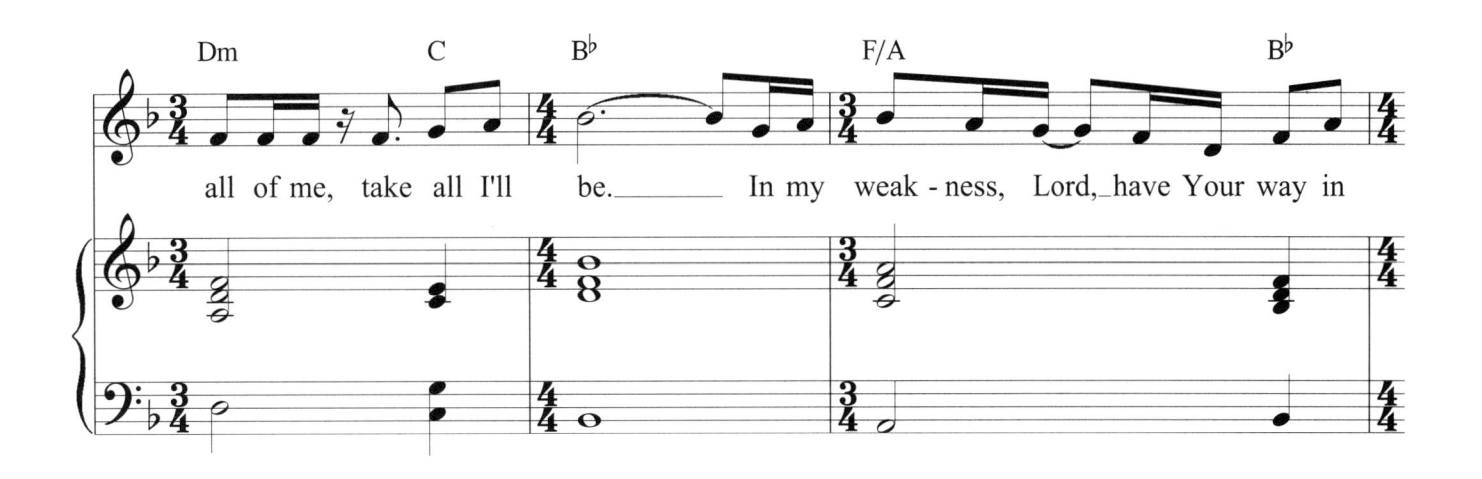

all of me, take all I'll be. In my weak-ness, Lord, have Your way in

1. me. To
2. me. Please walk be-

D.S. al CODA

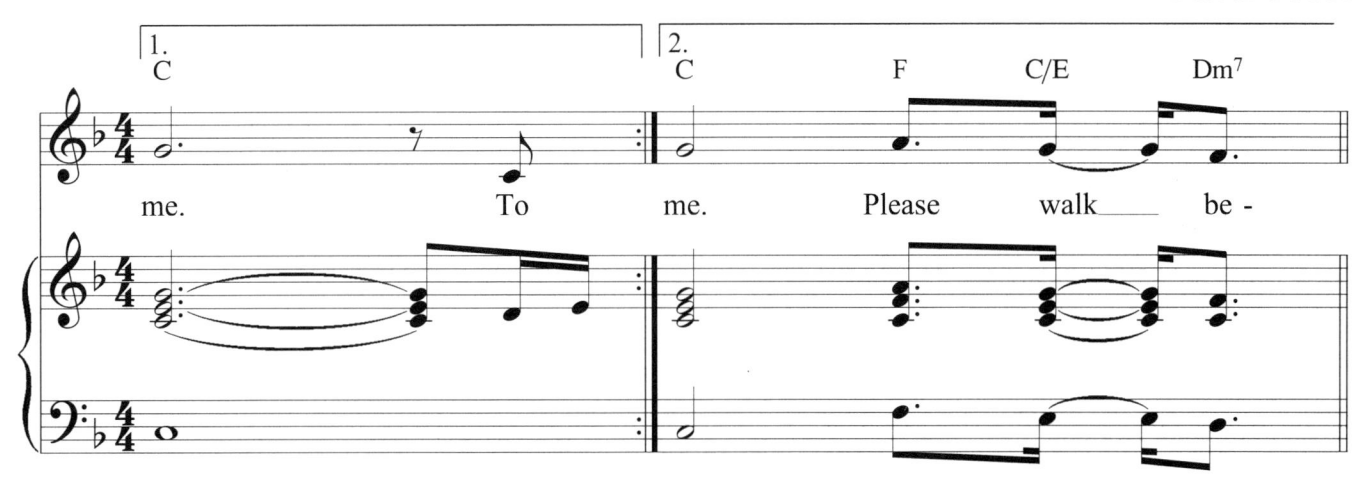

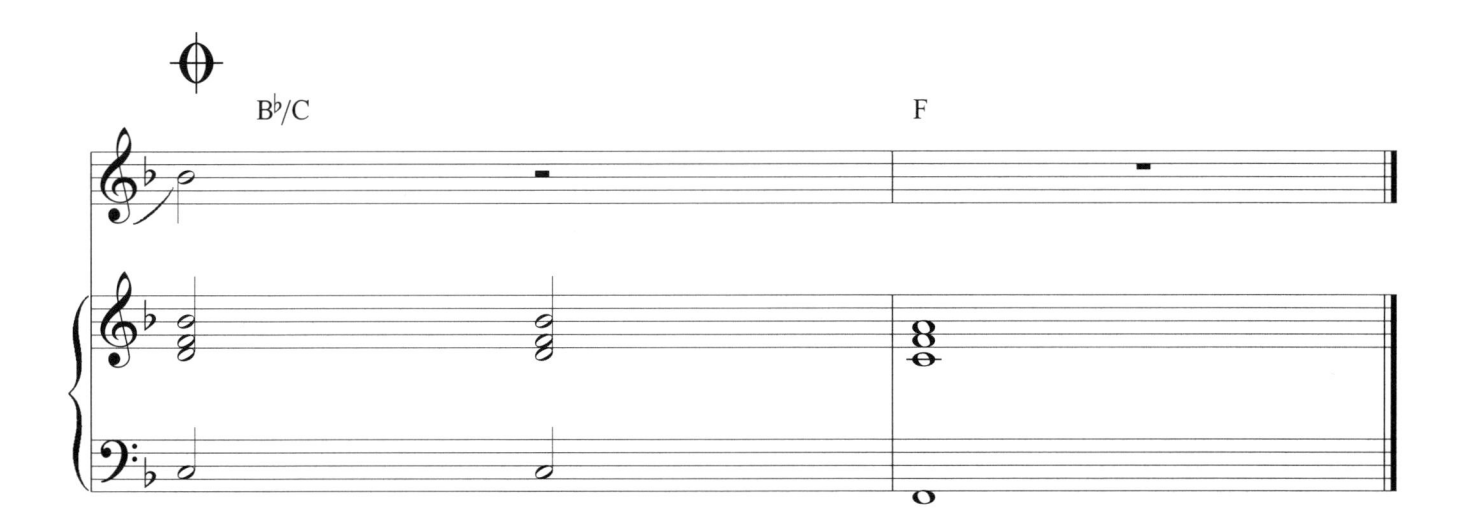

Bb/C F

Praise Him

Key of Am

♩=110

Words and Music by
Mark Naea and Vernon Katipa

From the Here to Him Music release: "Adore"(Parachute Band)

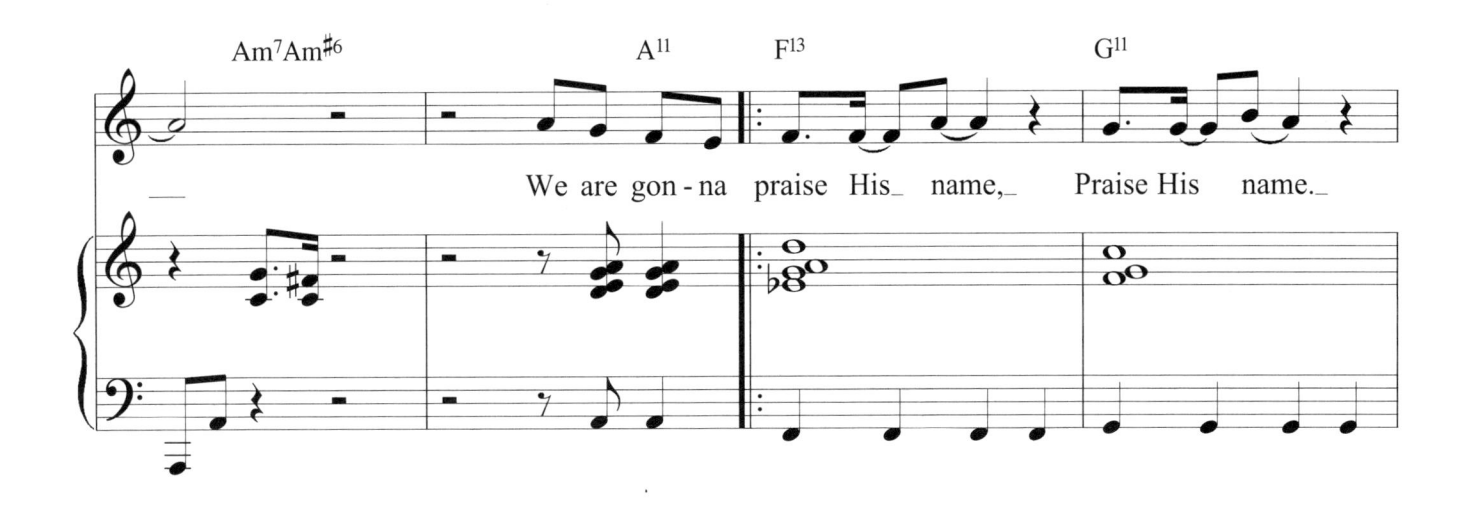

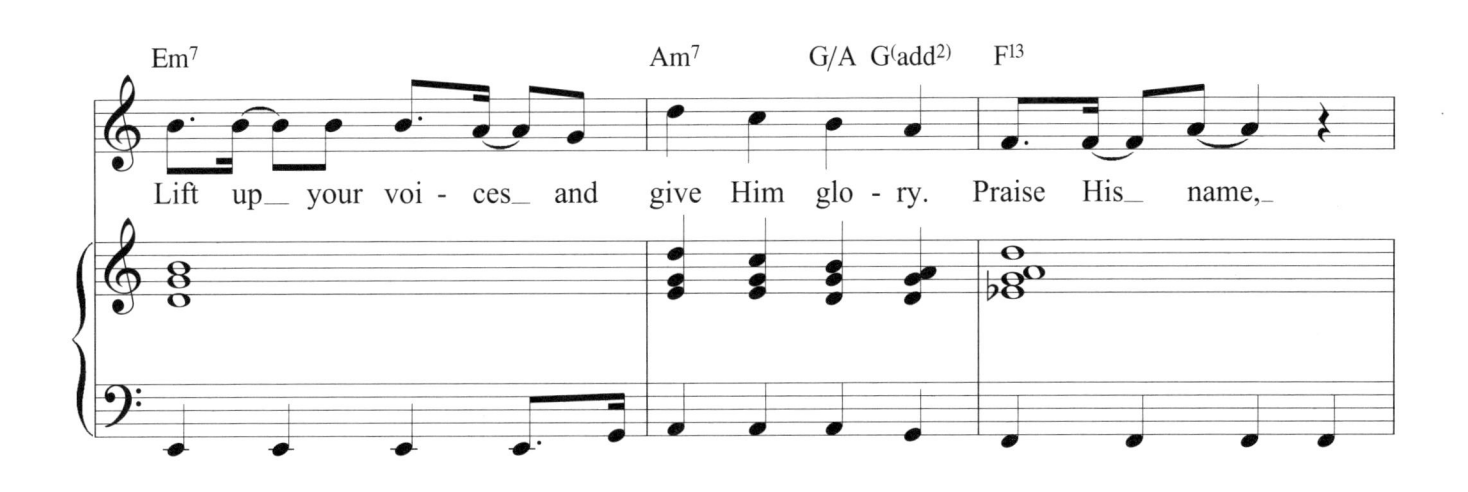

We are gon-na praise His name,_ Praise His name._

Lift up_ your voi-ces_ and give Him glo-ry. Praise His_ name,_

Praise His_ name_ on high._ We are gon-na

113

Pure and Holy

Key of Ab
♩=66

Words and Music by
Jamie Burgess

Let ev'ry thing that is-n't pure in Your sight, Lord Je-sus, be swept a-way by Your po-wer, Lord. I want to stand be-fore You dressed in the fin-est lin-en. Ho-ly in pu-ri-ty, my Lord. Pure and ho-ly, Giv-ing glo-ry

From the Here to Him Music release: "Always and Forever"(Parachute Band)
© 1998 Parachute Music, Admin. in the U.S. and Canada by Howard Publishing, Inc., West Monroe, LA (BMI)
www.worshipextreme.com

to the King of kings. Here be-fore You I a-dore You, Prais-es I will bring.

Radiance

Key of Am
♩=90

Words and Music by
Gavin Paton

I'm in love with You, You make my heart sing. I'm in love with You, You make my heart sing. And the more of You I know my love grows and grows and grows.

1. Let me
2.

From the Here to Him Music release: "Always and Forever" (Parachute Band)
© 1998 Parachute Music, Admin. in the U.S. and Canada by Howard Publishing, Inc., West Monroe, LA (BMI)
www.worshipextreme.com

Show me the radiance of Your glory. Em-power my life with Your love.

Rain Down

Key of C#m
♩=106

Words and Music by
Jason Harrison and Darin Sasser

Rain down all a-round. Pour in-to the cracks of this thirst-y ground. Give life to what was once con-si-dered bar-ren. Send it down, Your rain re-fresh-es, Lord. Heal-ing's found in Your rain, in Your rain. Send it down, Your rain re-fresh-es, Lord. Heal-ing's found in Your rain.

From the Here to Him Music release: "Among Thorns" (Among Thorns)
© 1998 ShadowRock Publishing Group, Admin. in the U.S. and Canada by Howard Publishing, Inc., West Monroe, LA (BMI)
www.worshipextreme.com

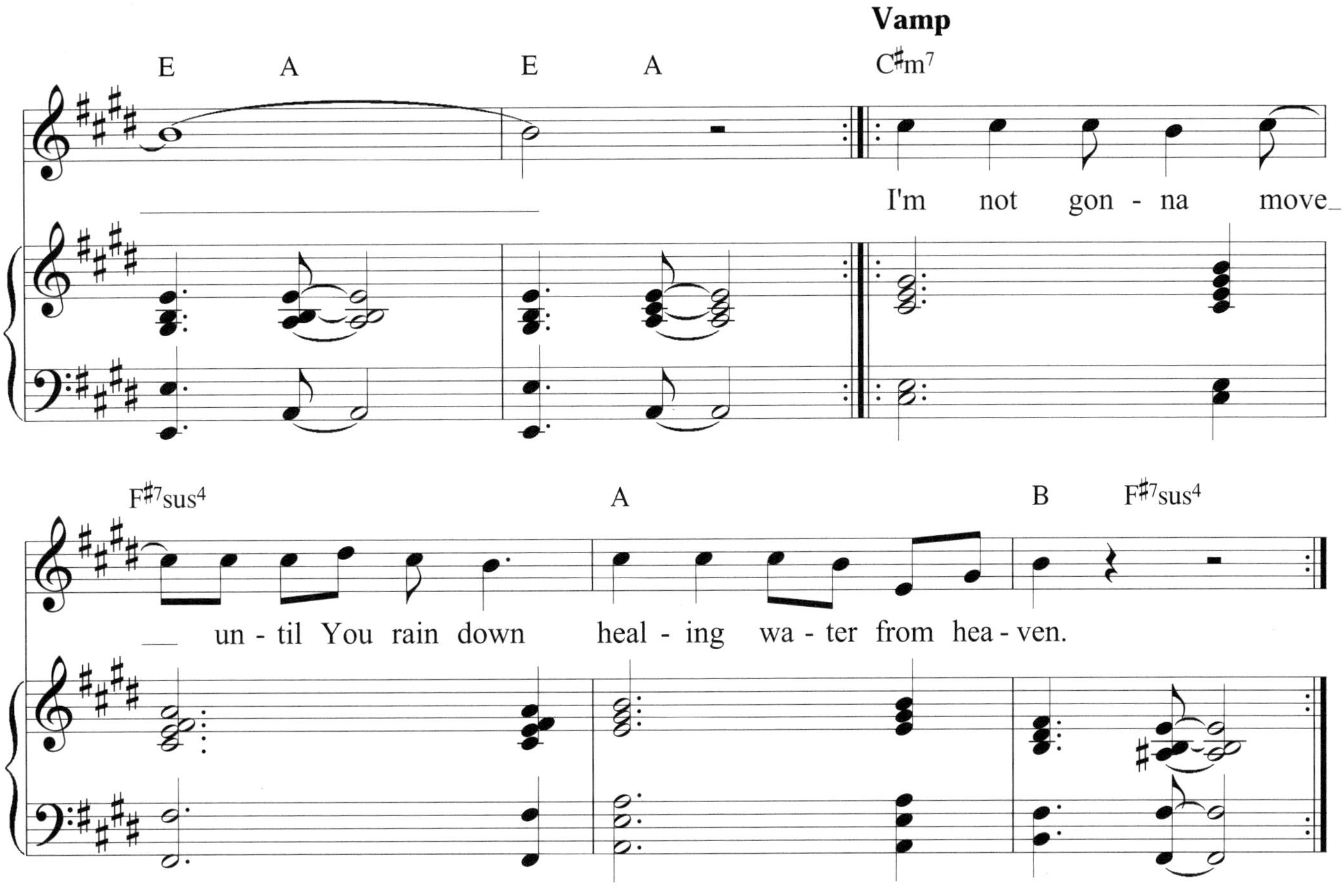
Vamp
E A E A C♯m7
I'm not gon - na move
F♯7sus4 A B F♯7sus4
until You rain down heal - ing wa - ter from hea - ven.

Redemption Day

Words and Music by Dean Rush

Key of D
♩=63

Li-be-rate, and Re-lease the chains, and Wipe the tears from my eyes. Free the slaves, and My cap-tive days and Wipe the tears from my eyes. I will walk a-way from sin In re-demp-tion day, yeah.

From the Here to Him Music release: "Journey Closer"(Form)
© 1999 Parachute Music, Admin. in the U.S. and Canada by Howard Publishing, Inc., West Monroe, LA (BMI)
www.worshipextreme.com

I will live my life with You in that day.

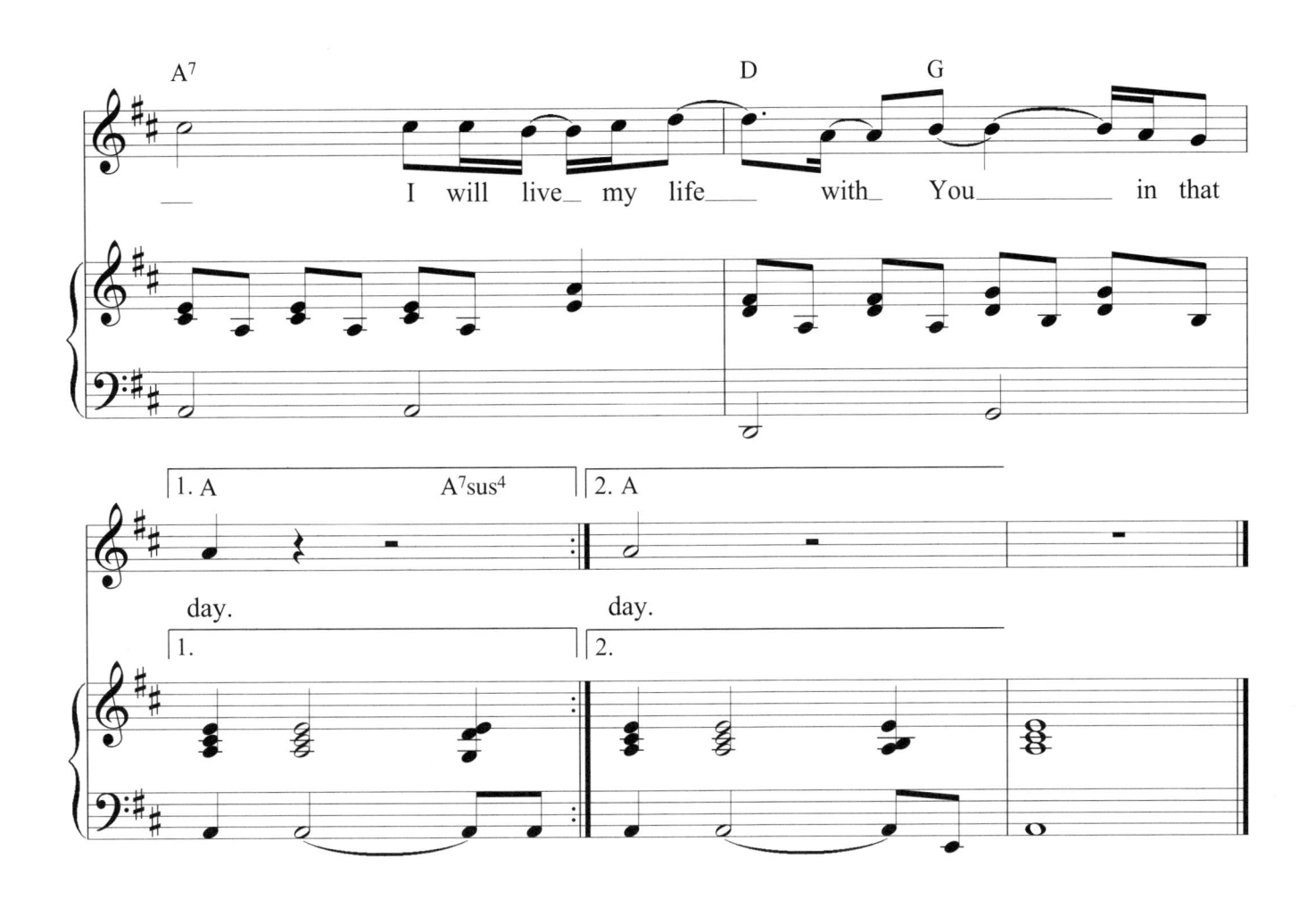

Key of G

♩=85

Rise Up

Words and Music by
Jason Harrison and Darin Sasser

From the Here to Him Music release: "Among Thorns"(Among Thorns)

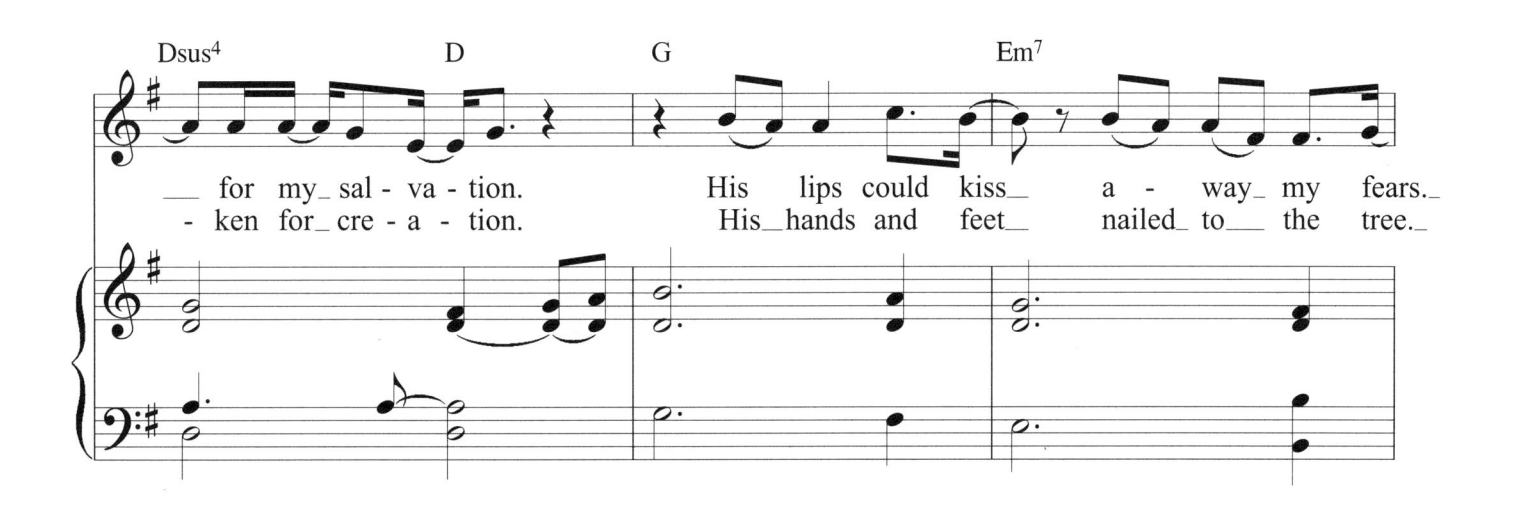

His heart bleeds love,_ pure_ self-less love._ His eyes_ cry tears_
God sent His Son,_ His_ on-ly Son,_ One_ bo-dy, bro-

_ for my_ sal-va-tion. His lips could kiss_ a-way_ my fears._
-ken for_ cre-a-tion. His_ hands and feet_ nailed_ to_ the tree._

_ His_ hands_ hold tight_ and ne-ver let_ me go._
_ Re-demp-tion found_ its way_ to you_ and me._

Shelter Me

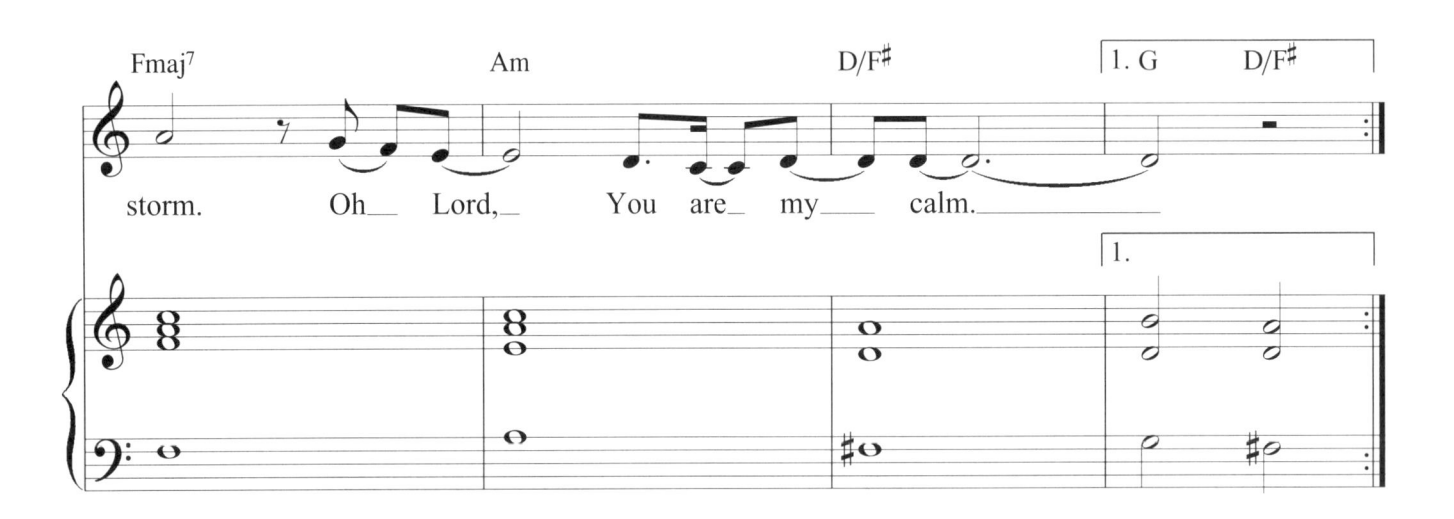

Key of C
♩=111

Words and Music by
Jason Harrison and Darin Sasser

You, oh Lord, are a harbor, a harbor from the storm. Oh Lord, You are my calm.

1. Shelter me, Wrap Your loving

From the Here to Him Music release: "Among Thorns"(Among Thorns)
© 1998 ShadowRock Publishing Group, Admin. in the U.S. and Canada by Howard Publishing, Inc., West Monroe, LA (BMI)
www.worshipextreme.com

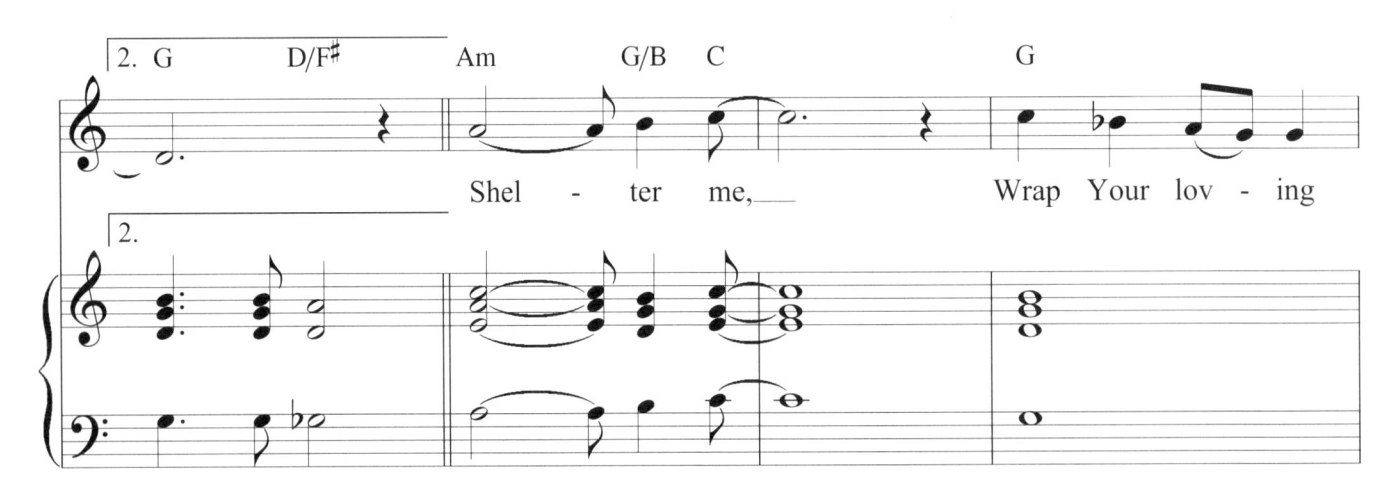

arms a-round me. Shel - ter me,___ Let Your wings of

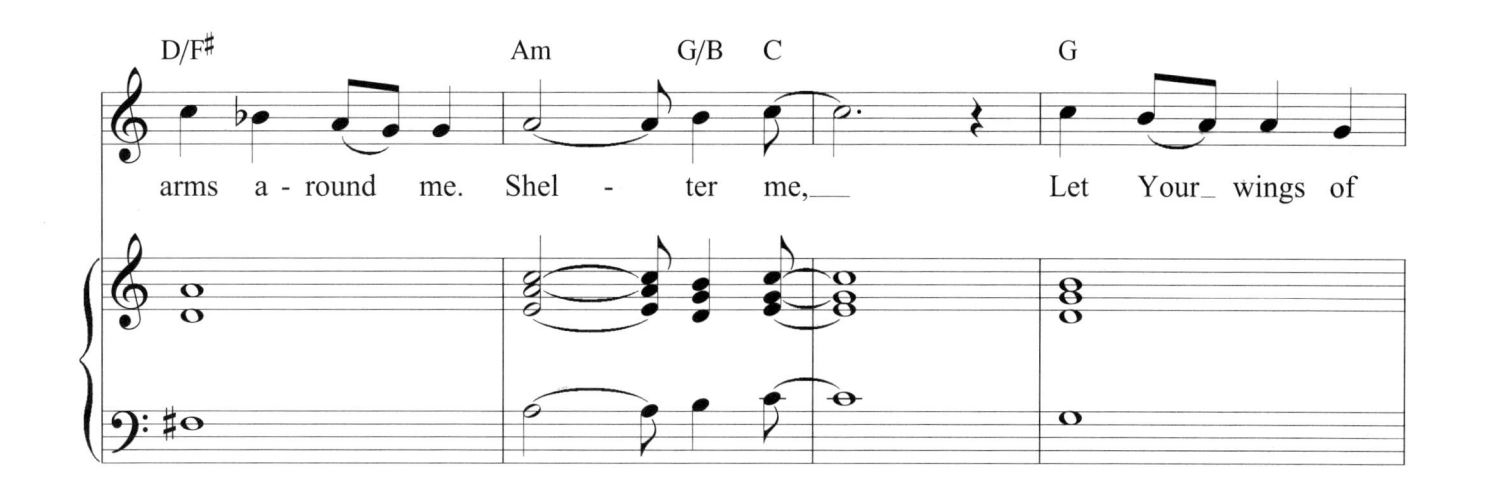

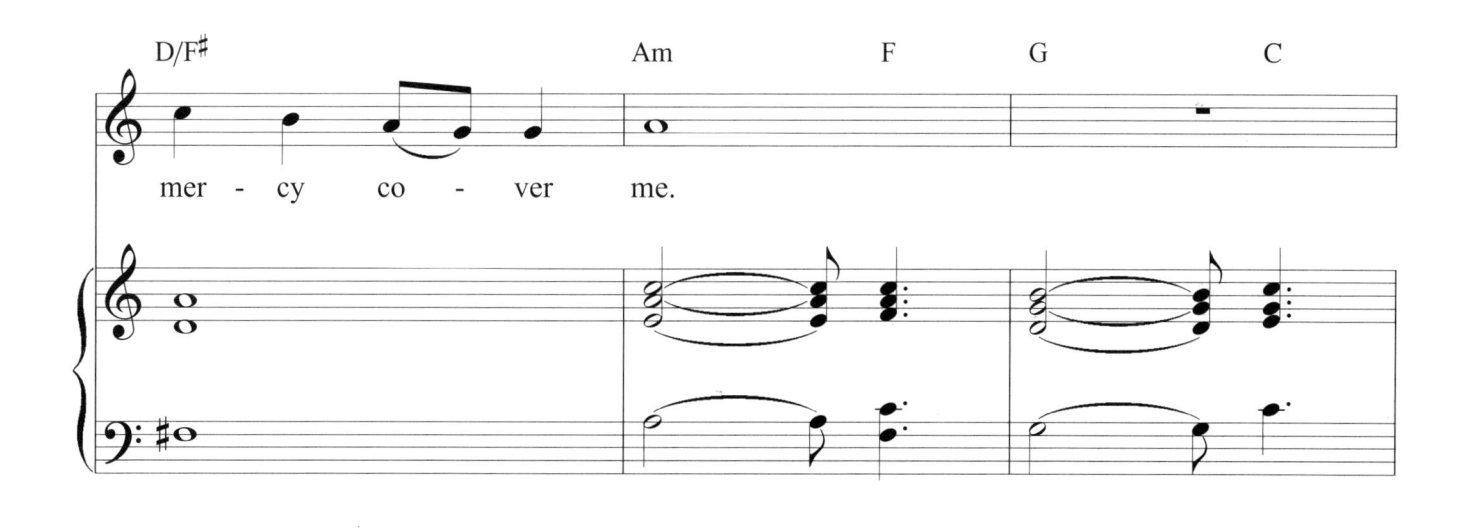

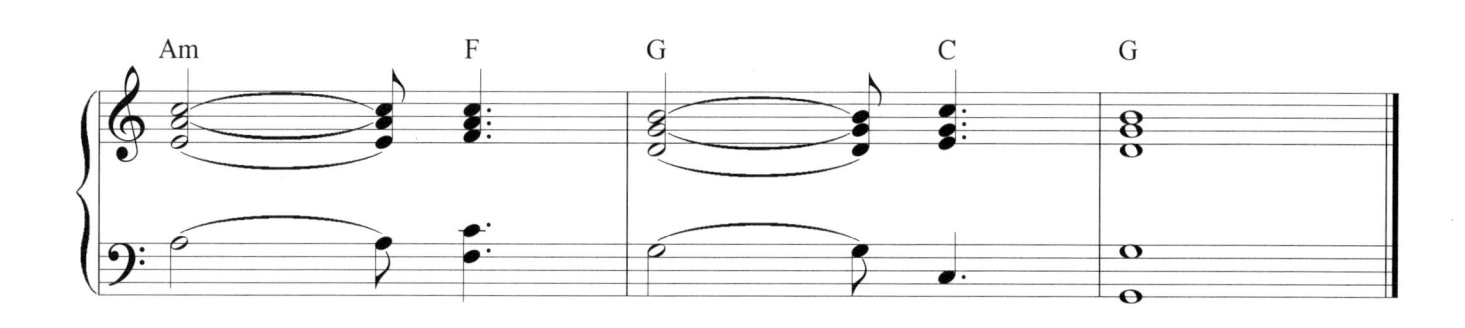

mer - cy co - ver me.

Key of Dm
With a swing

Shout It

Words and Music by
Louis Collins

From the Here to Him Music release: "Love"(Parachute Band)

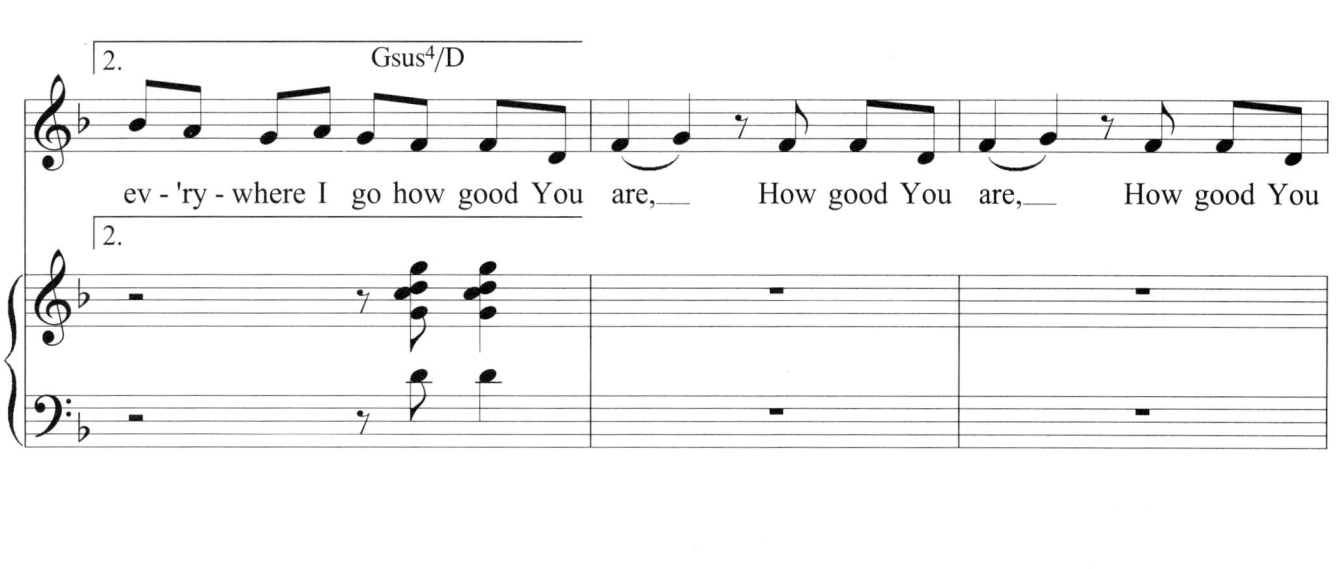

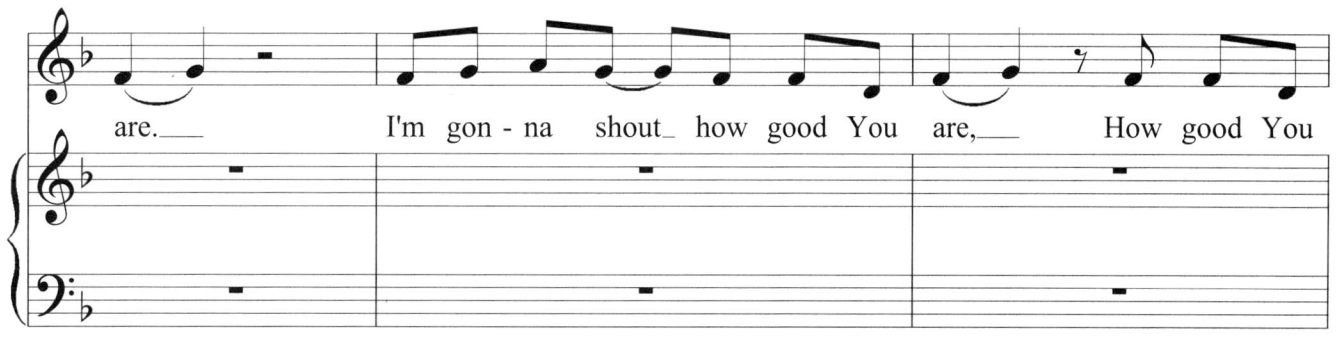

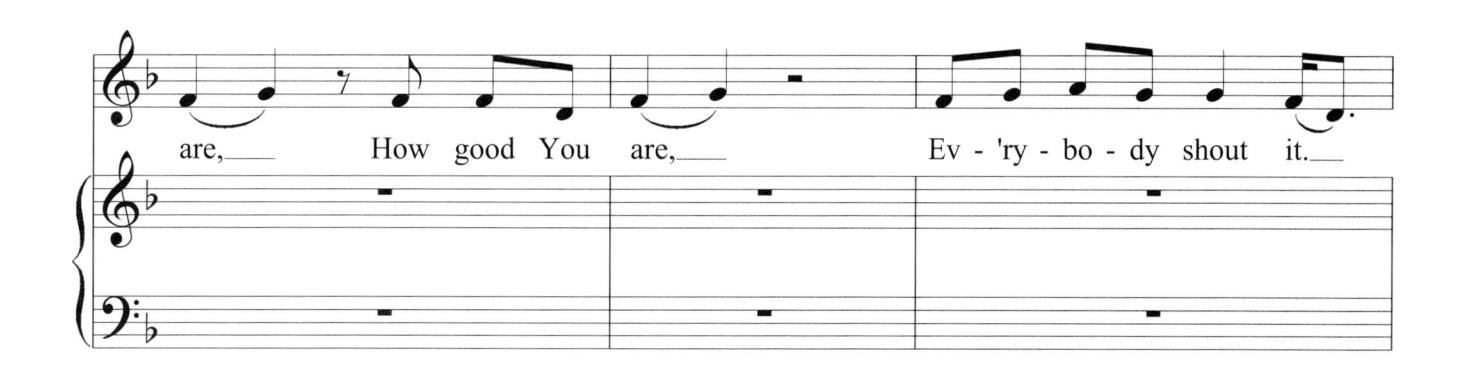

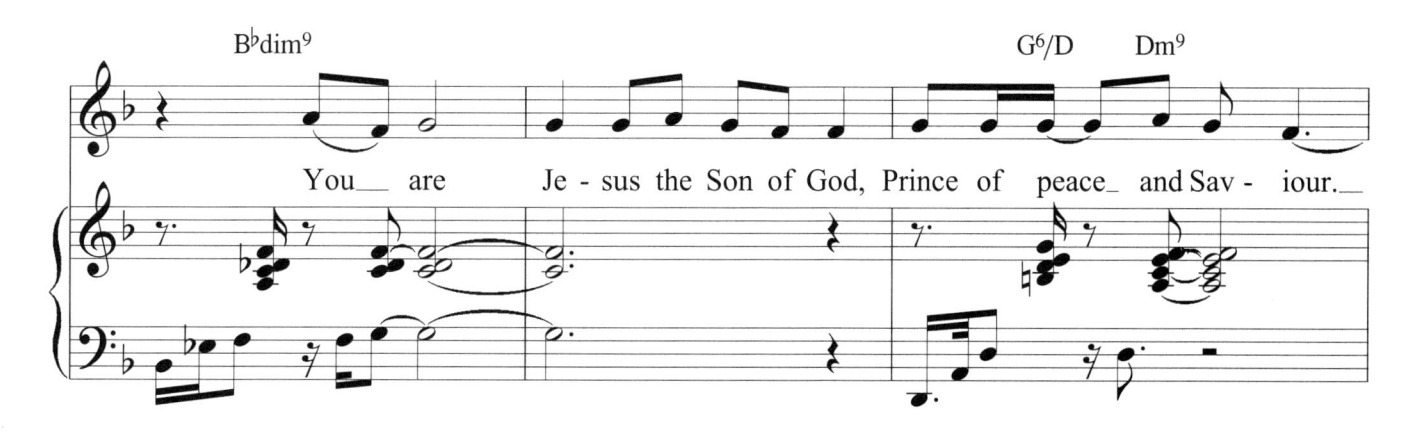

ev-'ry-where I go how good You are, How good You are, How good You are. I'm gonna shout how good You are, How good You are, How good You are, Ev-'ry-bo-dy shout it. You are Jesus the Son of God, Prince of peace and Saviour.

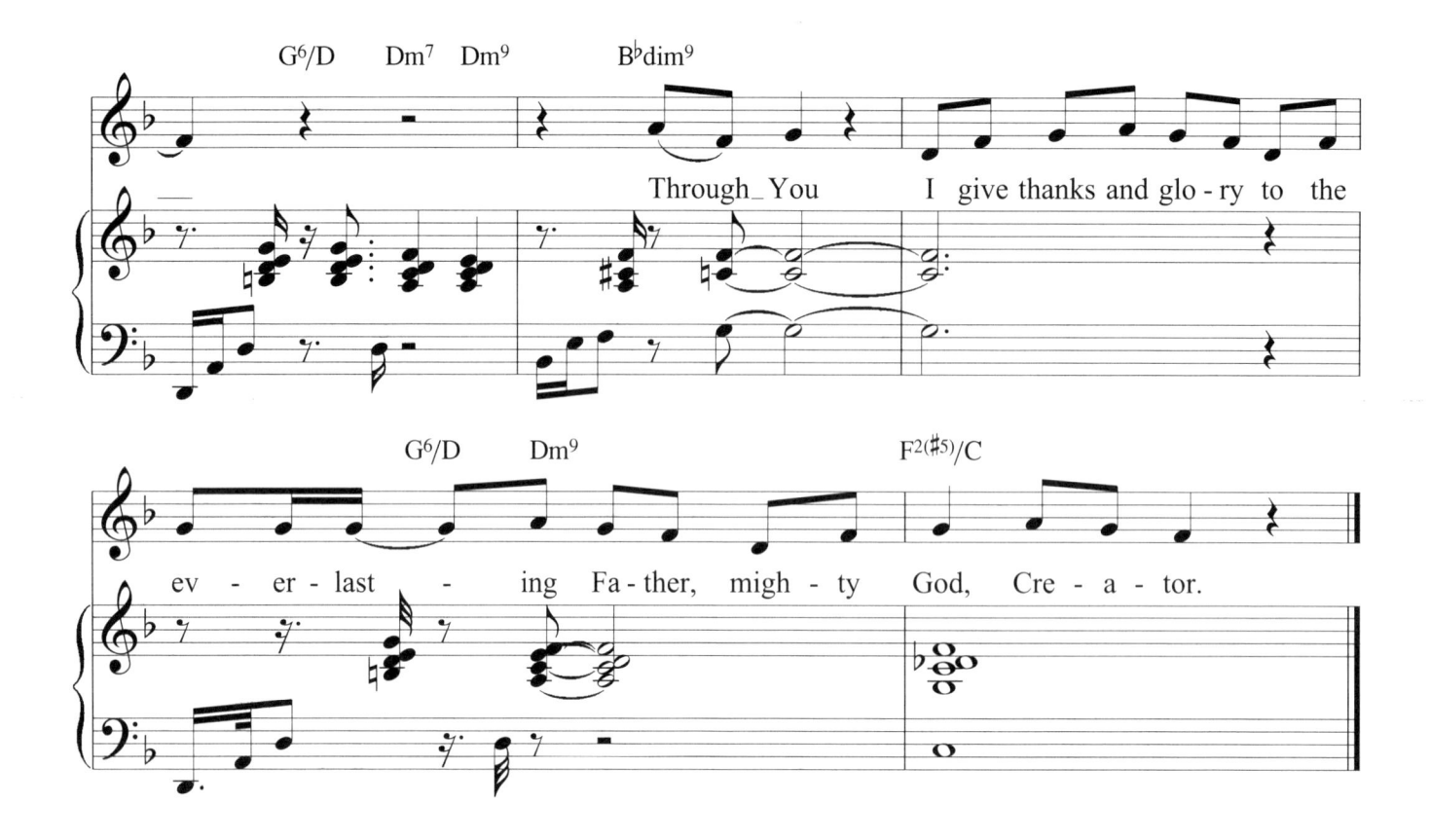

Through You I give thanks and glory to the ever-lasting Father, mighty God, Creator.

So Glad

Key of Cm
♩=118

Words and Music by
Chris de Jong

Cm7 — Dm7(add4) — E♭6 — F(add2)

Woh___ Woh___ Woh_ oh___

Cm7 — Cm7(add4) — E♭6 — F(add2)

So glad_ to call You Fa-ther._ So glad to call You friend.___

A♭maj9 — B♭9 — D♭maj9 — Dm7(♭5) G7♭6

So glad I can re-ly on,_ So glad_ I can de-pend on

FINE

Cm9 — Fm7 — Cm7

You_ You're my_ Pro-tec-tor,_ my on-ly Shel-ter._
You're my_ Re-deem-er, my Sav-ior,_ my Teach-er._

From the Here to Him Music release: "Adore"(Parachute Band)
© 1998 Parachute Music, Admin. in the U.S. and Canada by Howard Publishing, Inc., West Monroe, LA (BMI)
www.worshipextreme.com

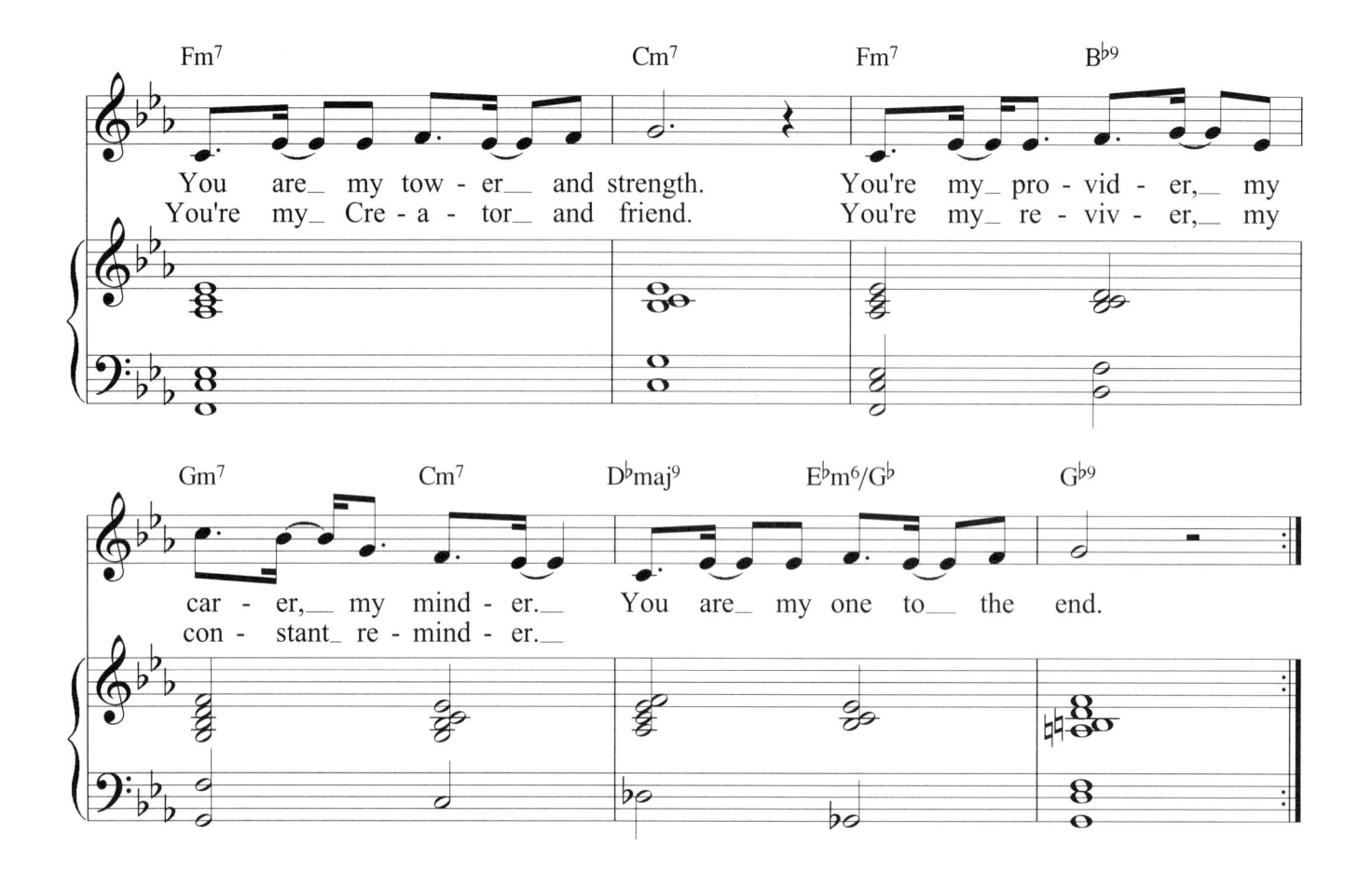

You are_ my tow - er_ and strength. You're my_ pro - vid - er,_ my
You're my_ Cre - a - tor_ and friend. You're my_ re - viv - er,_ my
car - er,_ my mind - er._ You are_ my one to_ the end.
con - stant_ re - mind - er._

Spirit Come

Key of F

Words and Music by
Jamie Burgess

We make the stand. We arise to see this land in revival. We pray down walls of satan' reign, Spirit rise in us again. We make the gain. Lord, we call out to Your Spirit. Lord, we call out to Your Spirit, And we cry out for this nation. We ask

From the Here to Him Music release: "You Alone" (Parachute Band)
© 1997 Parachute Music, Admin. in the U.S. and Canada by Howard Publishing, Inc., West Monroe, LA (BMI)
www.worshipextreme.com

"Come, Spirit come." We desire to see New Zealand as a nation living for You. Lord, we cry out for revival. We ask, "Come, Spirit, come." We make the

CODA *4 X*

"Come, Spirit, come."

Start a Fire

Key of F

Words and Music by
Jason Harrison and Darin Sasser

♩=80

Start a fire___ in me.___ Let the flames___ run free.___

Burn a-way___ the dross,___ ho-ly fire___ of God.___

Start a fire___ in me, Let the flames___ run free.___

Burn a-way___ the dross,___ ho-ly fire___ of God.___

From the Here to Him Music release: "Among Thorns"(Among Thorns)
© 1998 ShadowRock Publishing Group, Admin. in the U.S. and Canada by Howard Publishing, Inc., West Monroe, LA (BMI)
www.worshipextreme.com

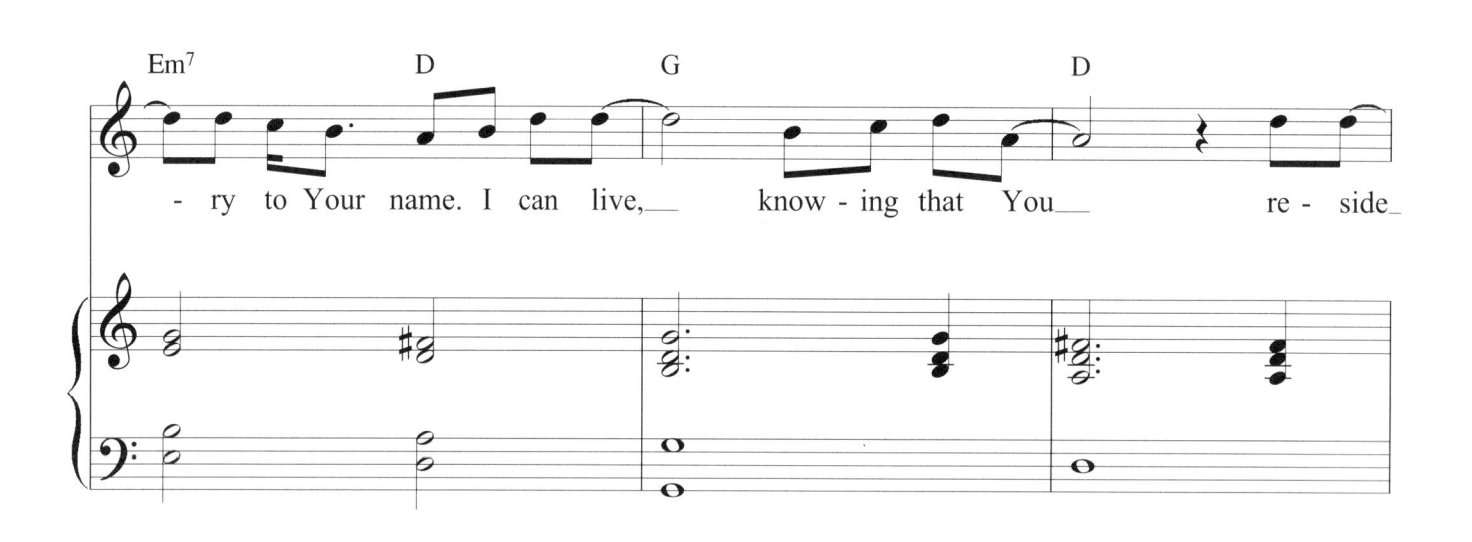

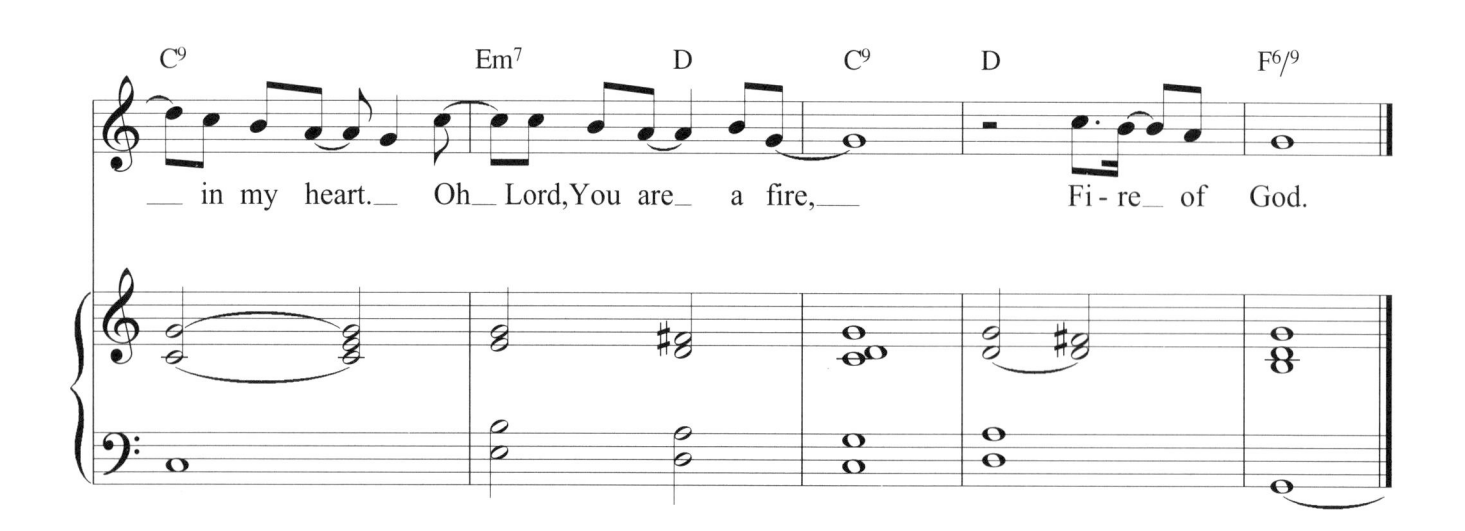

So let it be-gin, Let it be new. Let me be used for Your sake, Giv-ing glo-ry to Your name. I can live, know-ing that You re-side in my heart. Oh Lord, You are a fire, Fi-re of God.

Thank You, Jesus

Key of G

Words and Music by
Wayne and Libby Huirua

We're here to thank You Jesus.

We'll thank You all our days. For what You've done and what You'll do, we'll shout and celebrate in You.

Last x to CODA

We're here to thank You Jesus.

From the Here to Him Music release: "You Alone" (Parachute Band)
© 1997 Parachute Music, Admin. in the U.S. and Canada by Howard Publishing, Inc., West Monroe, LA (BMI)
www.worshipextreme.com

You've invited us to be with You.

Saying, "people, freely come"

What a privilege to praise our King.

We're here to thank You, Lord, Without hearts

we'll glad-ly sing.

We thank You (For the) hope and the vi-sion You have plan-ted in our hearts.

D.C. al CODA — CODA

137

Touch Me, Lord

Key of C
♩=72

Words and Music by
Louis Collins

Please hear my prayer, Lord. I seek Your presence. Come by Your Spirit 'Cause I'm hungry for You. I reach out for You. Oh Lord, please touch me. My heart's so hungry. Lord, it's

From the Here to Him Music release: "Love" (Parachute Band)
© 1999 Parachute Music, Admin. in the U.S. and Canada by Howard Publishing, Inc., West Monroe, LA (BMI)
www.worshipextreme.com

hun-gry for You._ Touch me, Lord,_ I'm wait-ing_ for a touch_ from You, Lord._ Ho-ly Spi-rit_ fall_ on_ me. Touch me, Lord_ I'm wait-ing_ for a touch_ from You, Lord._ Ho-ly Spi-rit,_ fall_

140

141

Wait On You

Key of A
♩=70

Words and Music by
Dean Rush

My frame was there before You As I was made in Your secret place. You looked upon my un-formed body And wrote the days You set for my life. I will wait for You. I will stay.

From the Here to Him Music release: "Journey Closer"(Form)
© 1999 Parachute Music, Admin. in the U.S. and Canada by Howard Publishing, Inc., West Monroe, LA (BMI)
www.worshipextreme.com

I will wait, Wait on You,

Wait on You.

You alone have searched me, You know my thoughts before I speak a word. You have laid Your hand upon me.

143

This is the place I am created for.

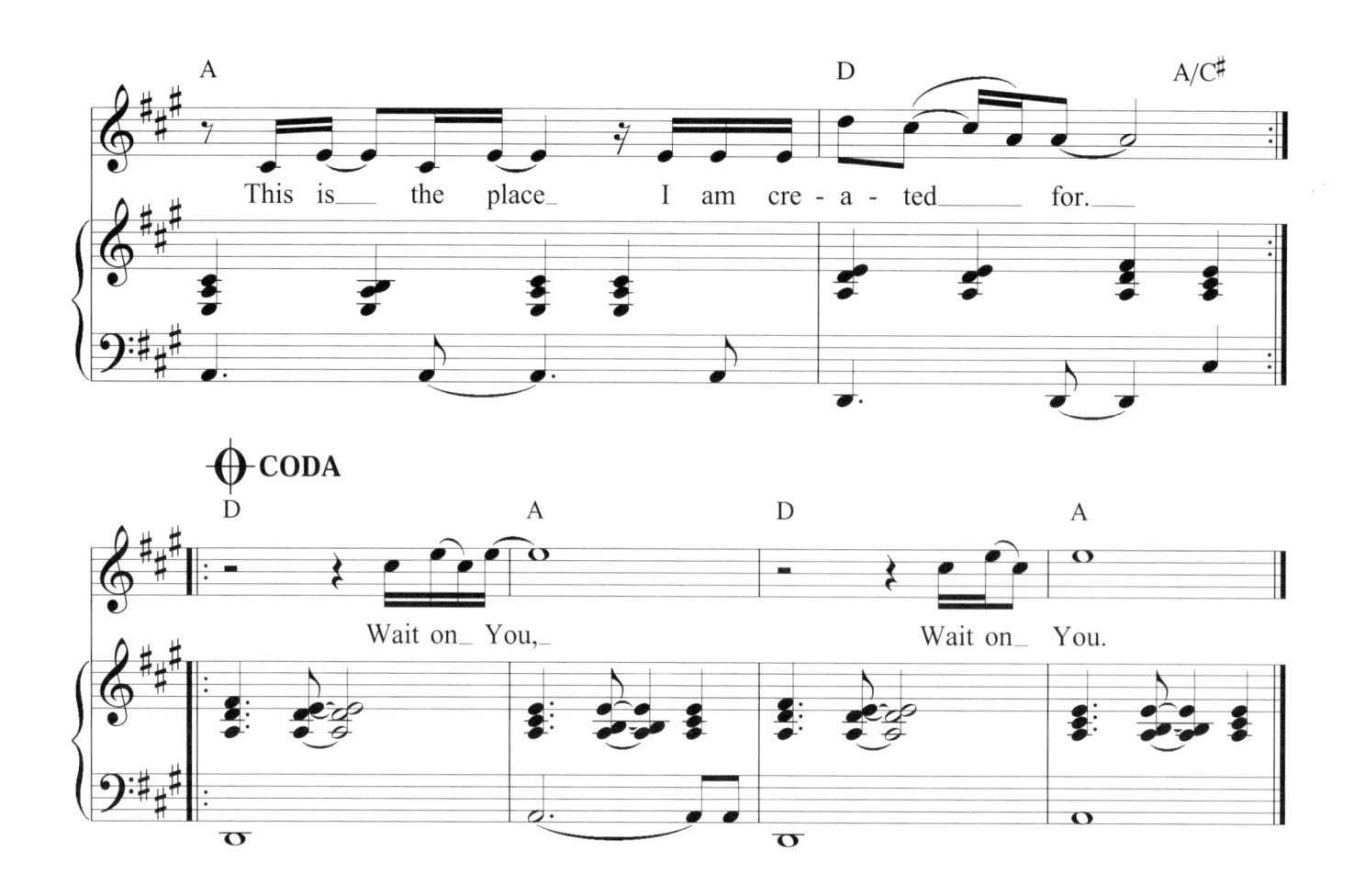

CODA

Wait on You, Wait on You.

We Seek Your Face

Key of Am

Words and Music by
Bonnie Low

Not power or glory, not ministry or fame, Not ableness or eloquence, not titles or name, Not fire or miracles, not thunder or rain, We seek Your face.

Not crowns or kingdoms, not houses or land. Not passion of pleasure, not blessings from Your hand. Not earthly inheritance, or richest reward,

We seek Your face.

From the Here to Him Music release: "You Alone" (Parachute Band)
© 1997 Parachute Music, Admin. in the U.S. and Canada by Howard Publishing, Inc., West Monroe, LA (BMI)
www.worshipextreme.com

We seek Your face.

Not All that we are and ever hope to be, we lay in at Your feet in worship, Poured out to You as a living sacrifice in worship, in worship to

You._____ (We seek Your) face,_____ We seek Your face._____ We seek Your (face) No pow'r or glory, seek Your face._ No crowns or kingdoms, seek Your face._ No passion pleasure, seek Your face._ We seek Your blessing, seek Your face.

Where Can I Go?

Key of G

Words and Music by
Dave Green

Where can I go to find You? What path must I travel down? I can't hide this love that I have, I've got to sing about the love I've found. You to me are everything I ever need. In my eyes I see nothing but You.

From the Here to Him Music release: PARACHUTE BAND *YOU ALONE*
© 1997 Parachute Music, Admin. in the U.S. and Canada by Howard Publishing, Inc., West Monroe, LA (BMI)
www.worshipextreme.com

With-in my heart You'll stay, Walk be-side me eve-ry day. There's no great-er love than Your love.

So I lift up my hands to You, sur-render my o-pin-ion to Your do-min-ion. Lord, I lift up my heart to You, give o-ver my in-ten-tions.

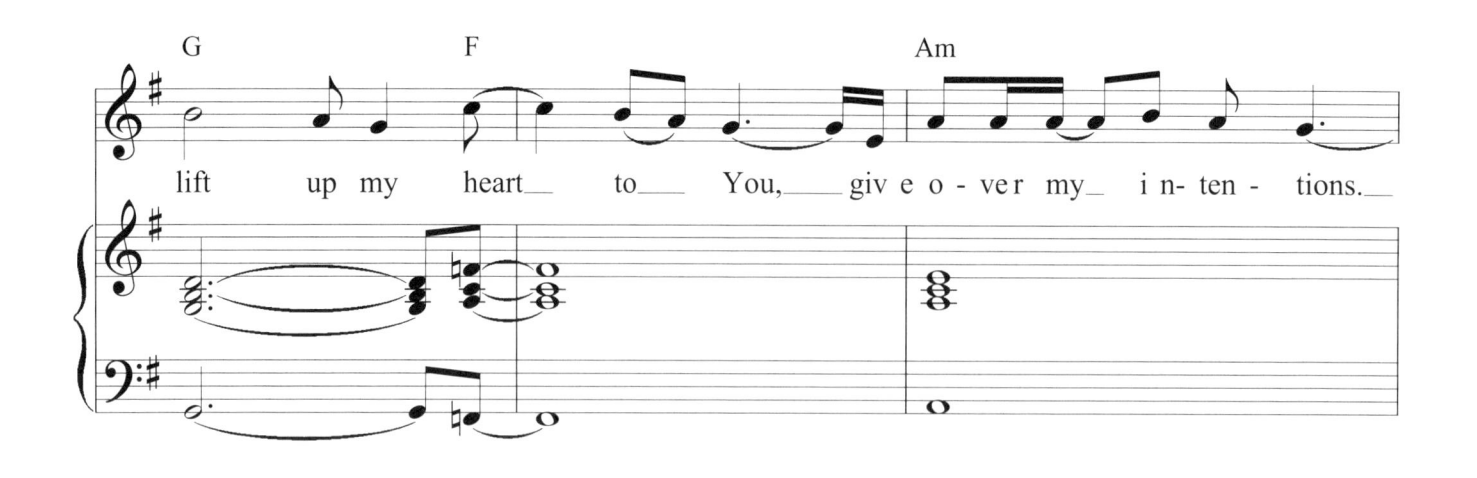

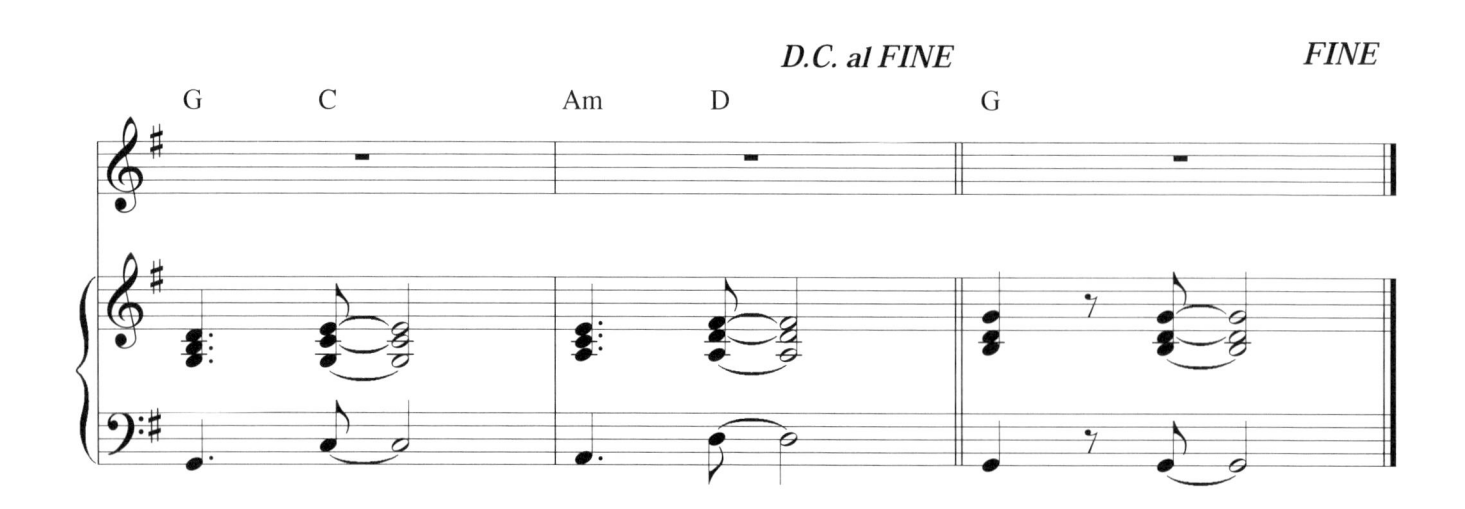

Your in-ter-ven-tion is what I need.

D.C. al FINE FINE

Without You

Key of G
♩=60

Words and Music by
Mark Naea, Vernon Katipa,
and Frank Kereopa

Lead me on, Holy Spirit, fill my heart, come flood my soul. Lead me on into Your presence. Touch me Lord, Jesus I need You. I can't live without You. I can't walk this

From the Here to Him Music release: "Adore" (Parachute Band)
© 1998 Parachute Music, Admin. in the U.S. and Canada by Howard Publishing, Inc., West Monroe, LA (BMI)
www.worshipextreme.com

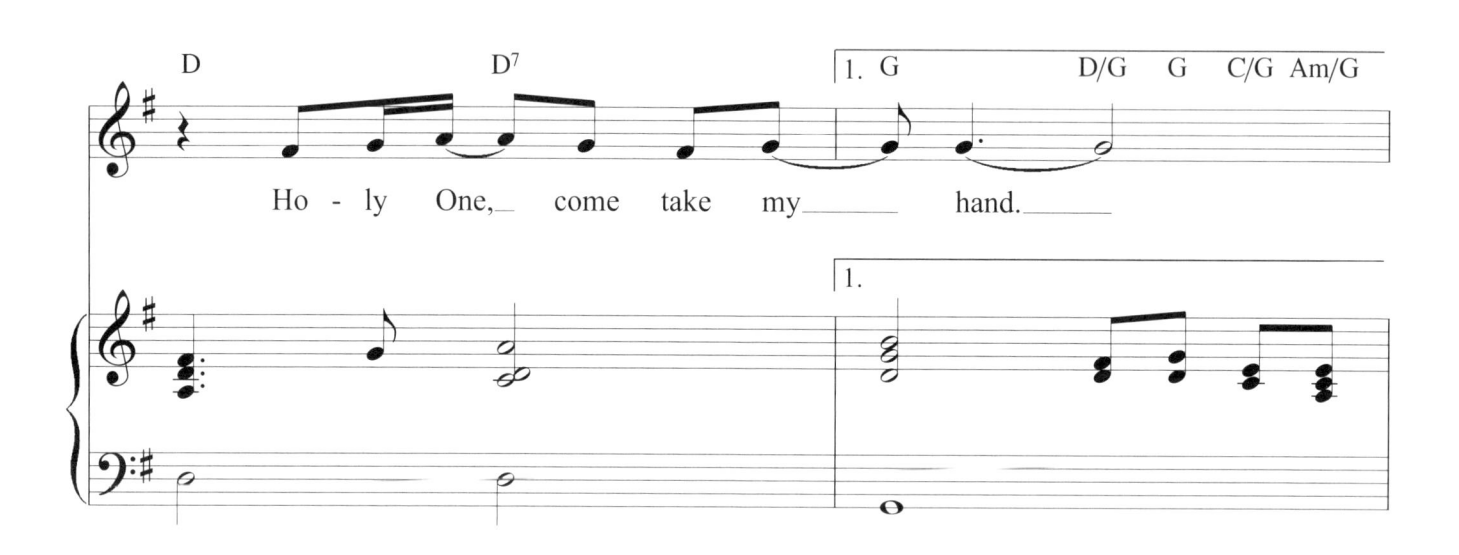

road a-lone. In my heart I need You. Ho-ly One, come take my hand. Lead me hand.

You Alone

Key of Am

Words and Music by
Wayne and Libby Huirua

All my life I'll praise You. There's no oth-er like You. You_ al-lone are Lord, Lord Je-sus.___ All my life I'll praise You. There's_ no oth-er like You. You_ a-lone are Lord, Lord Je-sus.___

Last x to CODA.

Who con-trols_ the rush-ing of_ the might-y wind?___
He is the One_ who holds_ the u - ni - verse.

From the Here to Him Music release: "You Alone" (Parachute Band)
© 1997 Parachute Music, Admin. in the U.S. and Canada by Howard Publishing, Inc., West Monroe, LA (BMI)
www.worshipextreme.com

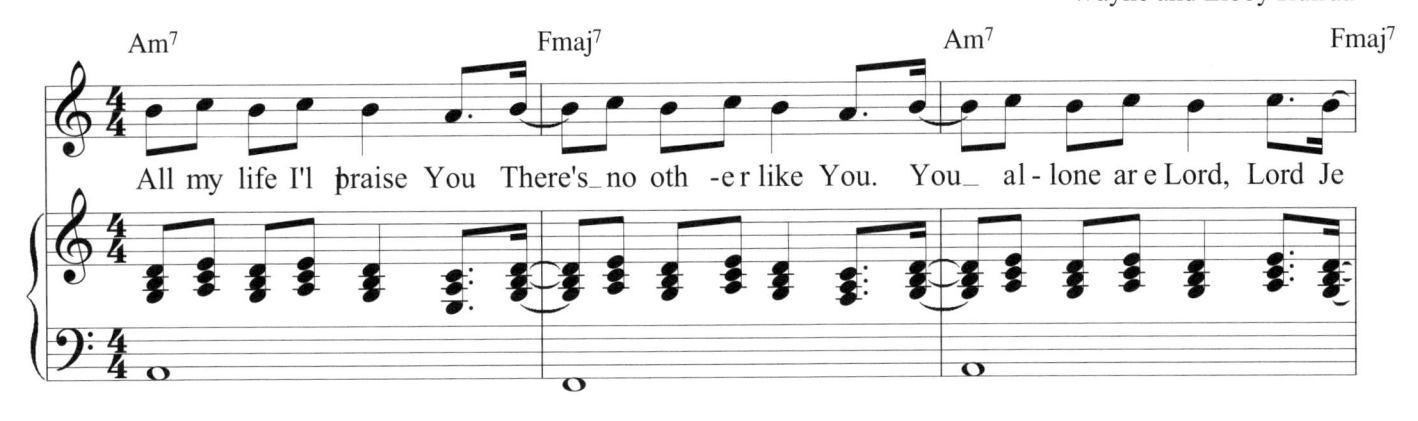

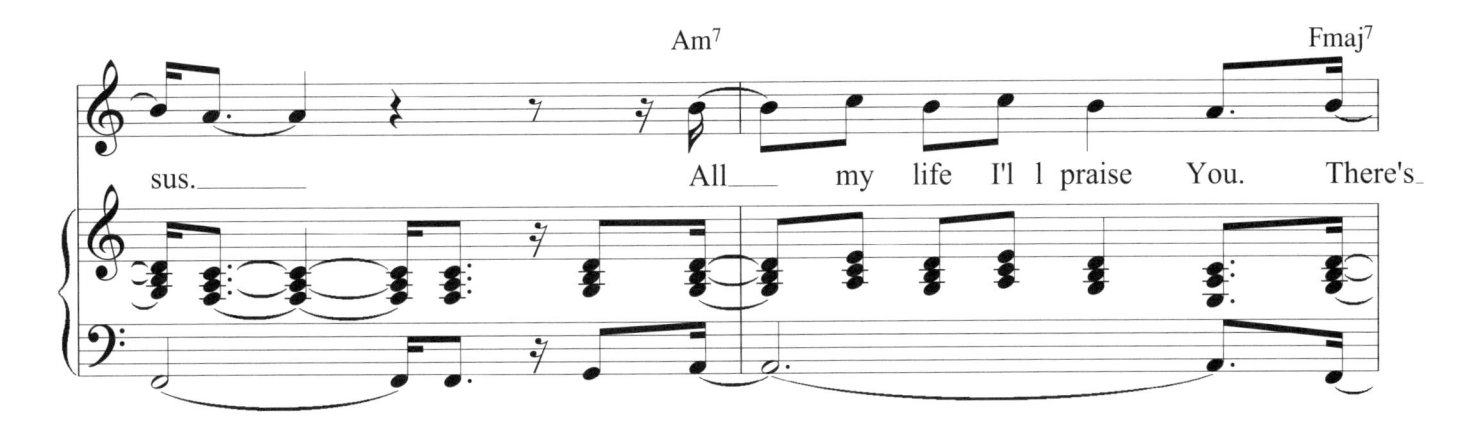

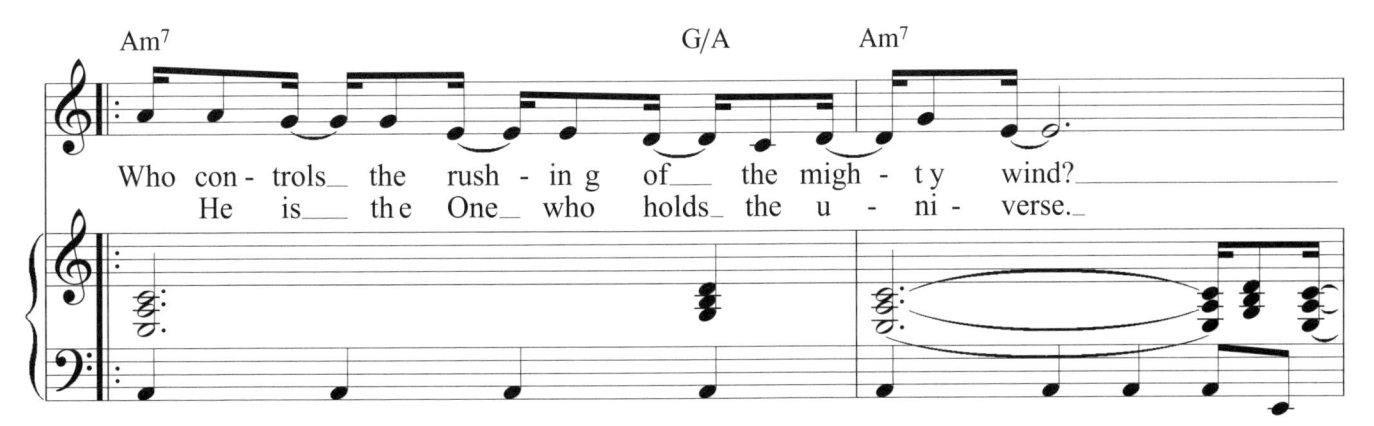

153

Who holds the power of the seas? Who by His word, formed the
The pow'r of life is in His hands. His strength is in me help-ing

hea-vens and the earth? Al-migh-ty God, The Lord
me to do His will. He is my Lord, In His

2nd X - D.C. al CODA

1. Je-sus is His name.
2. po-wer I will stand.

CODA

You a-lone are Lord. You a-lone are Lord, You a-lone are Lord, Lord Je

-sus. All my life I'll praise You, There's no other like You. You alone are Lord, Lord Jesus. All my life I'll praise You, there's no other like You. You alone are Lord, Lord Jesus. Lord Jesus, Lord Jesus.

You Are God

Key of Em

Words and Music by
Jason Harrison and Darin Sasser

♩=104

You are the Light, You are the Life, You are the Source of sal-va-tion, Fire by night. You are the voice I choose to heed. You are the Light, You are the

From the Here to Him Music release: "Among Thorns"(Among Thorns)
© 1998 ShadowRock Publishing Group, Admin. in the U.S. and Canada by Howard Publishing, Inc., West Monroe, LA (BMI)
www.worshipextreme.com

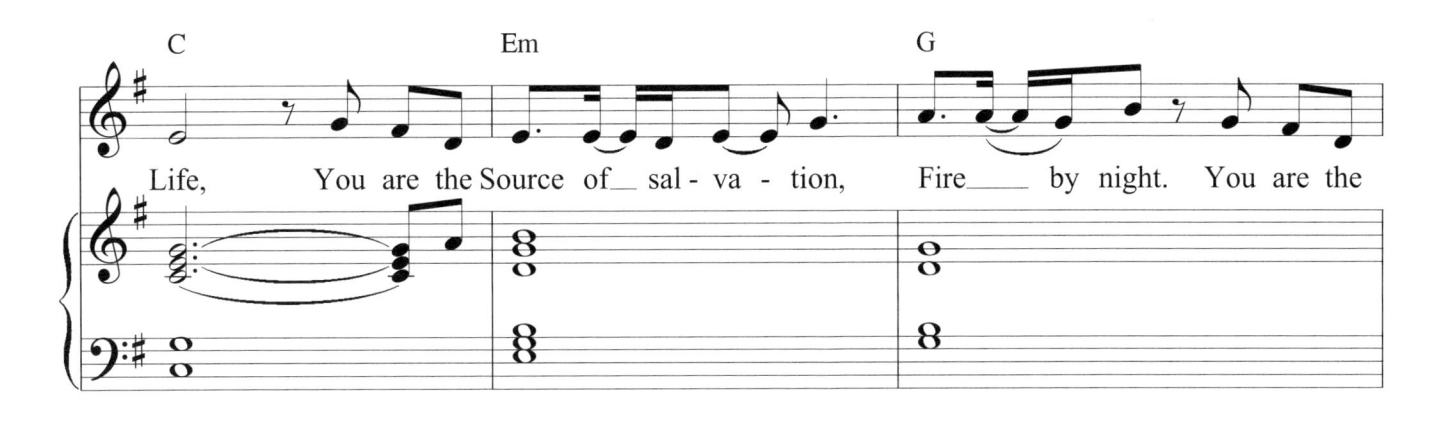

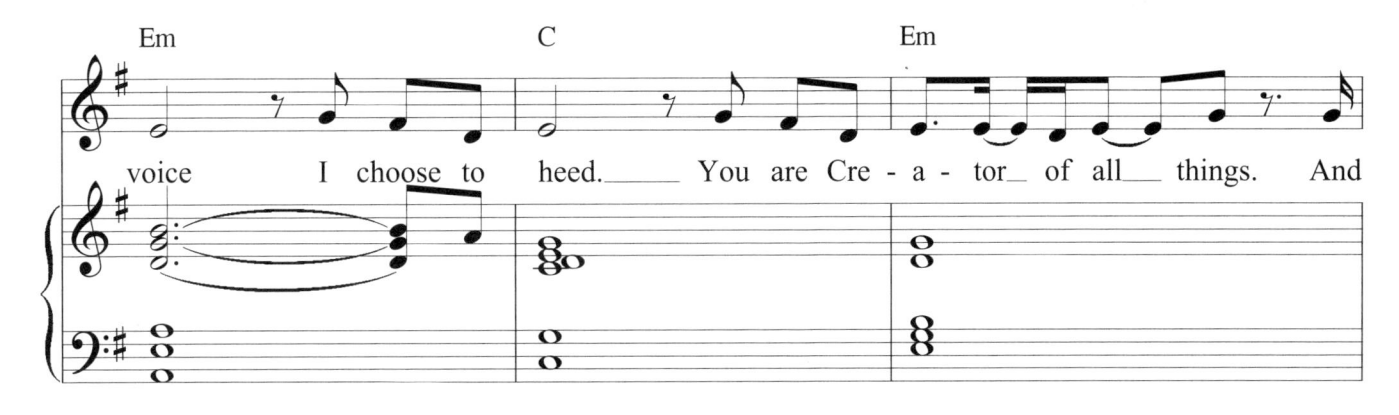

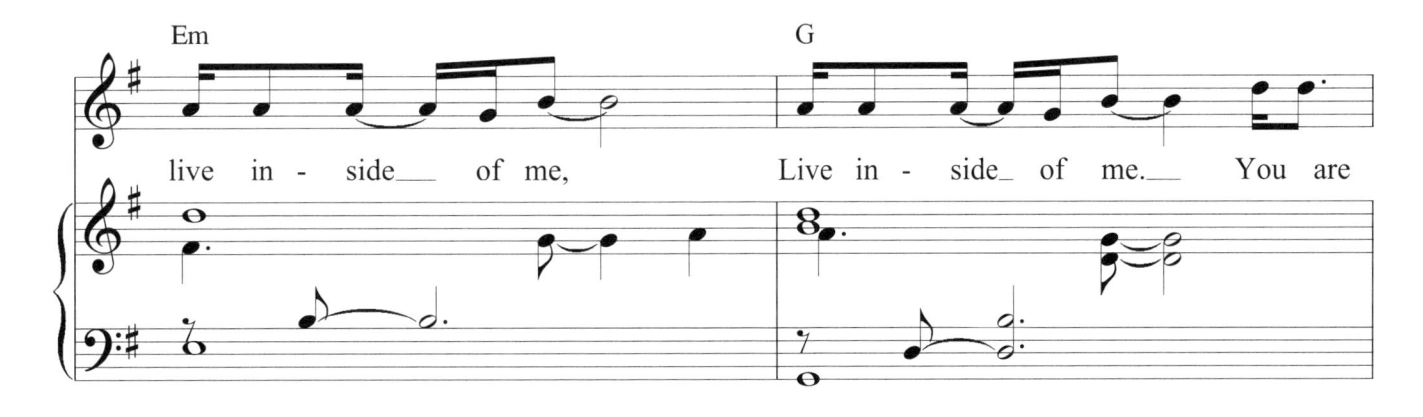

Life, You are the Source of salvation, Fire by night. You are the voice I choose to heed. You are Creator of all things. And You will meet my needs. You are God And You live inside of me, Live inside of me. You are

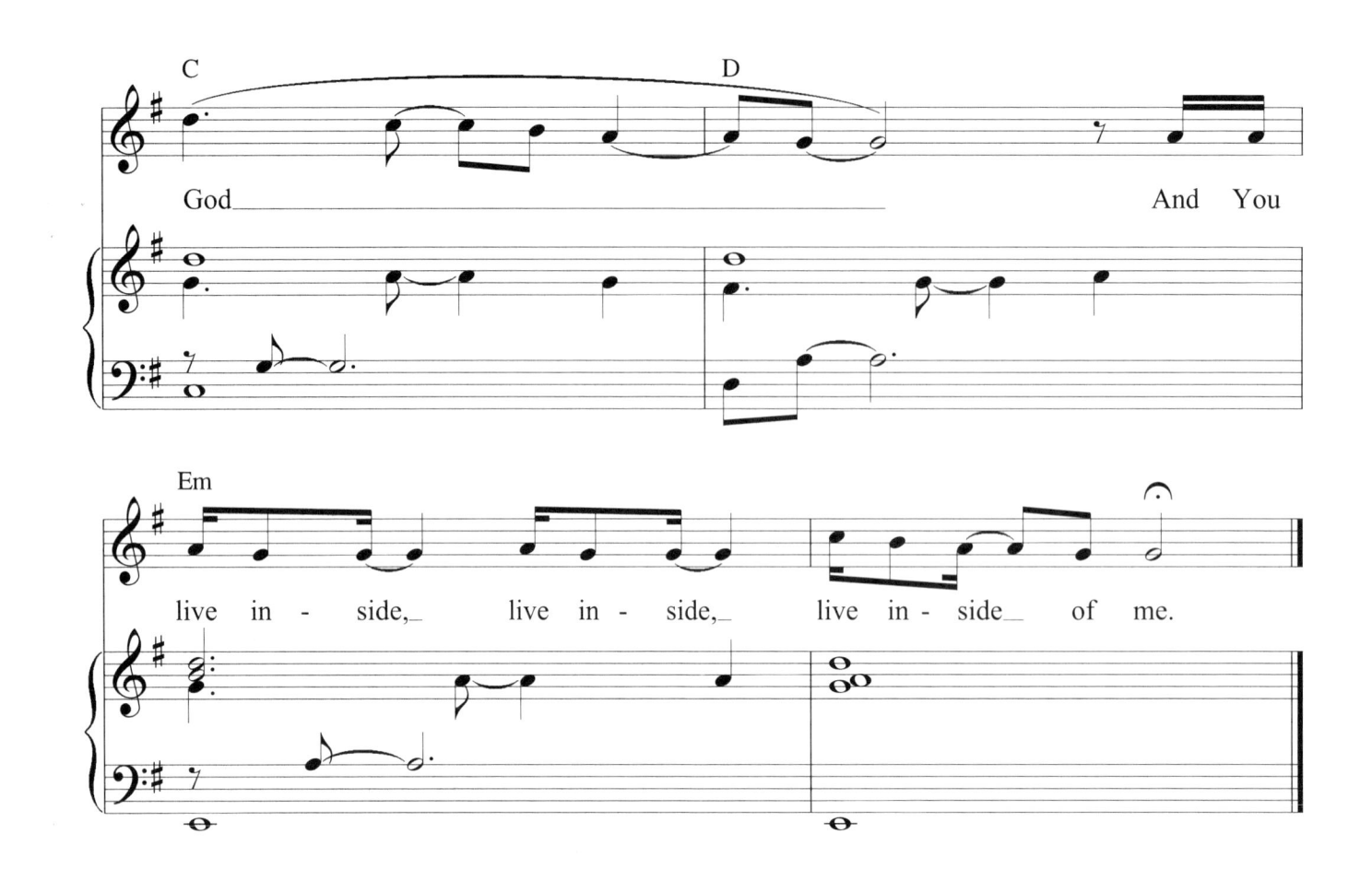

God_____ And You live in-side,_ live in-side,_ live in-side_ of me.

158

You Are God Alone

Key of A
♩=60

Words and Music by
Evan Silva

In Your pre-sence Lord, we come.
bow.
We're here to praise and worship You.
We're here to praise and honor You.
There is no one be-side You, none can com-pare to You
You are faith-ful to our way for-e-ver and a day.
or do the things You do.
To You I'll al-ways pray.
You are God a-lone
You have giv-en life

From the Here to Him Music release: "Always and Forever" (Parachute Band)
© 1997 Parachute Music, Admin. in the U.S. and Canada by Howard Publishing, Inc., West Monroe, LA (BMI)
www.worshipextreme.com

Your Spirit from above reveals to us Your love and gently guides us on.

Gently guides us on

1. To Your feet we come to
2. Gently guides us on.

Gently guides us on.

You Are Lord

Key of F
♩=63

Words and Music by
Ray Chee

You are Lord, Maker of the heavens. You are Lord, Ruler of all nations. I lift my voice to worship You, Lord.

You are Lord, Healer and Messiah. You are Lord, Wonderful Redeemer. I crown You King of Kings and Lord of Lords.

From the Here to Him Music release: "Adore" (Parachute Band)
© 1998 Parachute Music, Admin. in the U.S. and Canada by Howard Publishing, Inc., West Monroe, LA (BMI)
www.worshipextreme.com

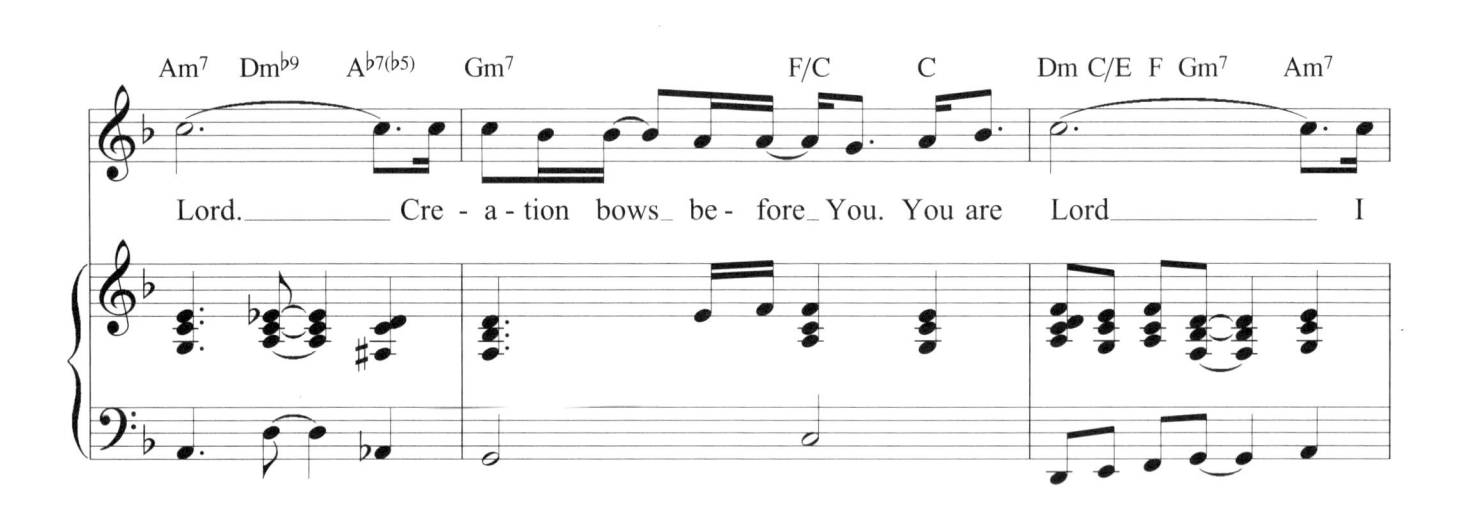

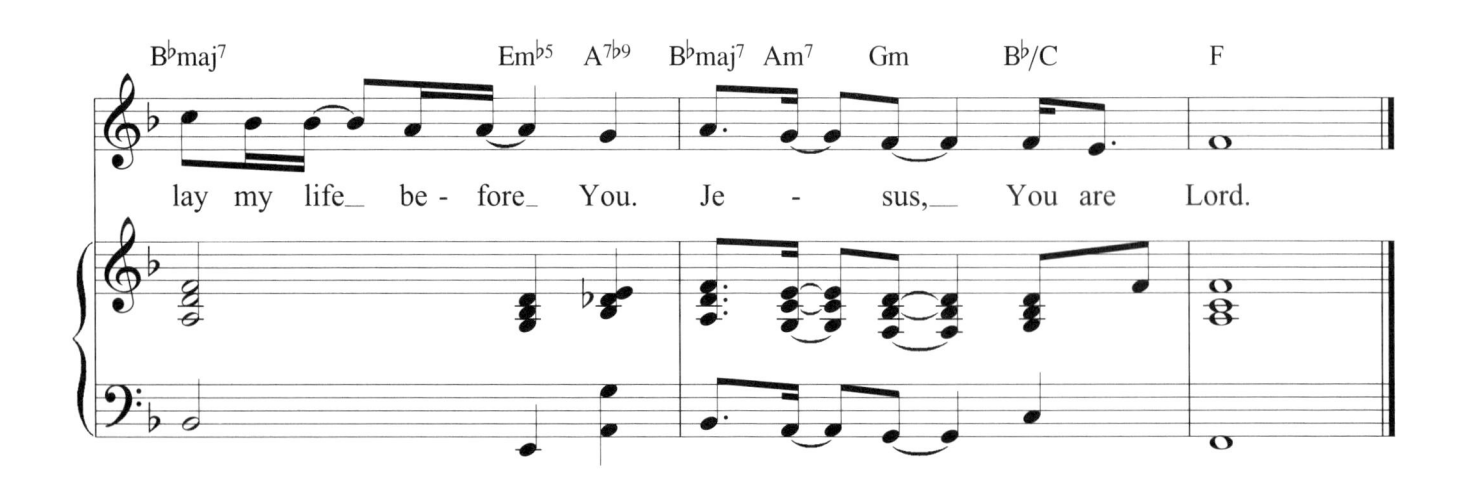

You are Lord. I worship and adore You. You are Lord. Creation bows before You. You are Lord. I lay my life before You. Jesus, You are Lord.

Key of G

You Make Me Free

Words and Music by
Dean Rush

♩=138

G/B   **C**   **G**

You start a fire within me.

G/B   **C**   **G**

I feel it's burning embers.

Bm7   **C**   **G**

A purifying water. (Save my soul.)

Em   **C**   **G**

Visions deep within me.

From the Here to Him Music release: "Journey Closer" (Form)
© 1999 Parachute Music, Admin. in the U.S. and Canada by Howard Publishing, Inc., West Monroe, LA (BMI)
www.worshipextreme.com

163

Bm7
C
G
You lift_ me,
I am changed._
Bm7
C
G
You lift_ me,
Arms of grace._
Bm7
C
G
You lift_ me,
I am free_
to - day._
D
G
C

| G/B | C | G | D/F# |

You make me free,___ And I am free__ to-day.__

| G/B | C | G | D/F# |

You make me free,_____ And in You I__ am saved.__

| Em | C | G | D/F# |

You make me free,__ And I__ stay._____

| G/B | C | G | D/F# |

You make me free._____

Key of F

You Mean Everything To Me

Words and Music by
Suzannd Su'a, Reupena
Su'a, and Anthony Cahya

You mean ev'-ry-thing to me, Lord, You are so faith-ful, Where I wan-na be is in Your pre-sence. You mean pre-sence. That's where I be-long. When Your Spi-rit's fal-ling on me, Where I feel strong, When Your grace is up-on me, You've

From the Here to Him Music release: "You Alone" (Parachute Band)
© 1997 Parachute Music, Admin. in the U.S. and Canada by Howard Publishing, Inc., West Monroe, LA (BMI)
www.worshipextreme.com

given me a song, and now I'm going to worship in Your presence.

1. You mean

2. I only want to live for You, Giving You glory in all that I do. You mean presence.

Your Love

Key of A
♩=74

Words and Music by
Louis Collins

Your love___ Is wa-ter un-to___ my soul.___
Is faith-ful and true___ to me.___

Your love___ Fills me and makes___ me whole.___
Is bet-ter than live___ to me.___

Your love___ It
soothes and it heals.___ Your love,___ E-ter-ni-ty seals. Your love.___
Bought li-ber-ty___ for all___ for e-ter-ni-ty___

From the Here to Him Music release: "Love" (Parachute Band)
© 1999 Parachute Music, Admin. in the U.S. and Canada by Howard Publishing, Inc., West Monroe, LA (BMI)
www.worshipextreme.com

Oh your love, Oh my heart How it longs,
It's longing for more and more of Your love. I belong,
Lord, to You. I'm longing for more and more of Your love.

1. Your love love
2. A